K9 AGGRESSION CONTROL

K9 Professional Training Series

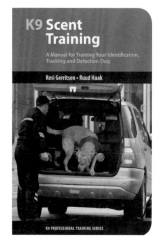

K9 Scent Training
A Manual for Training Your Identification, Tracking and Detection Dog
Resi Gerritsen • Ruud Haak
K9 PROFESSIONAL TRAINING SERIES

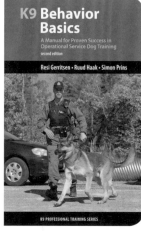

K9 Behavior Basics
A Manual for Proven Success in Operational Service Dog Training
second edition
Resi Gerritsen • Ruud Haak • Simon Prins
K9 PROFESSIONAL TRAINING SERIES

K9 Search and Rescue
A Manual for Training the Natural Way
second edition
Resi Gerritsen • Ruud Haak
K9 PROFESSIONAL TRAINING SERIES

K9 Drug Detection
A Manual for Training and Operations
Resi Gerritsen • Ruud Haak
K9 PROFESSIONAL TRAINING SERIES

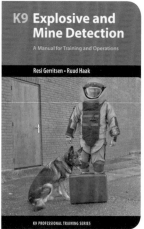

K9 Explosive and Mine Detection
A Manual for Training and Operations
Resi Gerritsen • Ruud Haak
K9 PROFESSIONAL TRAINING SERIES

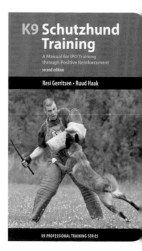

K9 Schutzhund Training
A Manual for IPO Training through Positive Reinforcement
second edition
Resi Gerritsen • Ruud Haak
K9 PROFESSIONAL TRAINING SERIES

See the complete list at
dogtrainingpress.com

K9 AGGRESSION CONTROL

Teaching the "Out"

SECOND EDITION

Dr. Stephen A. Mackenzie

K9 Professional Training Series

An imprint of
Brush Education Inc.

Brush Education Inc.
www.brusheducation.ca
contact@brusheducation.ca

Editorial: Meaghan Craven
Cover Design: John Luckhurst
Cover image: courtesy Lauren Anderson
Interior Design: Carol Dragich, Dragich Design
Photo credits: Lauren Anderson (figures 1.1–1.3, 3.5–3.7); James Cortina (figures 3.1–3.4); Lisa Brannon (figures 5.1–5.7, 6.1–6.10); John Johnston (figures 6.11–6.20).

Printed and manufactured in Canada

Library and Archives Canada Cataloguing in Publication
Mackenzie, Stephen A. (Stephen Alexander), 1948- [Aggression control] K9 aggression control: teaching the out / Stephen A. Mackenzie. — Second edition.

(K9 professional training series) Revision of: Aggression control : teaching the out / Stephen Mackenzie. — Calgary : Detselig Enterprises Ltd., ©2009. Issued in print and electronic formats.

ISBN 978-1-55059-706-6 (softcover).—
ISBN 978-1-55059-707-3 (PDF).—
ISBN 978-1-55059-708-0 (MOBI).—
ISBN 978-1-55059-709-7 (EPUB)

1. Dogs—Training. 2. Dogs—Behavior. 3. Aggressive behavior in animals. I. Title. II. Title: Aggression control. III. Series: K9 professional training series

SF431.M34 2017   636.7′0887   C2017-902761-1
                                                       C2017-902762-X

Dedication

To Rusty, a half-Labrador, half–Irish setter, who saved a young boy's life by retrieving him out of Lake Samamish, WA, in the early 1950s. Rusty is long gone now, but because of him the little boy grew up to write this book.

Contents

Acknowledgements

The author is indebted to the following: William Nott Jr., John Brannon, and Franco Angelini for sharing their personal adaptations of the author's original methods; and John Johnston of Ace K9, Lisa Brannon of Shallow Creek Kennels, Lauren Anderson of Equine Exposures, Franco Angelini, and James Cortina for providing photographs.

Disclaimer

While the contents of this book are based on substantial experience and expertise, working with dogs involves inherent risks, especially in dangerous settings and situations. Anyone using approaches described in this book does so entirely at their own risk and both the author and publisher disclaim any liability for any injuries or other damage that may be sustained.

Selecting the Correct Dog and the Yerkes-Dodson Law

Selecting the Correct Dog

Training a police dog is a large, multifaceted project. Unfortunately, on the very first day of this project, many trainers inadvertently and unconsciously doom themselves to failure by selecting the wrong type of dog. Good police dogs must be able to learn and solve problems when they are highly excited, and therefore, only dogs with the ability to think clearly when excited and quickly calm down when it is appropriate should be taken into training. Time and time again we see trainers testing canine candidates for confidence, environmental soundness, approachability, aggression, hunting behavior, and other important qualities and do nothing to evaluate the dogs' ability to keep a clear head and calm down quickly. This is regrettable, since these are the qualities that allow us to teach aggression control later.

> **Only dogs with the ability to think clearly when excited and quickly calm down when it is appropriate should be taken into training.**

There seem to be two major conditions for confident dogs with high levels of aggression: one, the aggression can be accompanied by a clear-headed attitude or, two, the aggression can be unreasonable and expressed when the dog is unprovoked and remain high even after the original provocation has ceased. Police dogs are supposed to react to how people behave not how they are dressed. If a dog flings himself aggressively at the decoy when the decoy is acting normally simply because the decoy is in a bite suit or wearing a sleeve, this is unprovoked aggression that will make extra work for us later. If the dog is uncontrollable in this situation, we will probably have trouble with impulse control later. When the aggression level of a dog remains high even after the stimulation for aggression has stopped, the dog is telling us as clearly as he can that he is going to give us control problems later. Unfortunately, many trainers see dogs like this and think they are "high in drive," score them highly, and pay money for them when in fact they are not superior candidates; they are simply wild animals that are not suitable for training to be a modern, approachable police dog. Please do not mistake the intent here; a high level of aggression is indeed necessary to produce a good police dog, but it is not enough by itself. We need a dog that is highly aggressive but also able to remain calm, to solve problems, and to learn new things in exciting situations. Calmness is a behavior, and it can be selected for and rewarded just like any other behavior. Unfortunately, very few trainers do this.

> **When the aggression level of a dog remains high even after the stimulation for it has stopped, the dog is telling us as clearly as he can that he is going to give us control problems later.**

TESTING FOR CALMNESS AND A CLEAR HEAD

There are several ways to test for calmness and a clear head, and if you already have a good method, you might want to stick with it. If you are inexperienced or have no favorite test, the following method will get you started.

Take the dog to a location he is not familiar with and have a person dressed in a bite suit or wearing a sleeve stand passively in the middle of the test area, not stimulating the dog in any way. If the dog is trained in obedience, do some on-leash obedience around the decoy to see if the dog can focus on the handler, even with the decoy near. If the dog cannot break his focus on the decoy to pay attention to the handler, the dog is reacting only to how the decoy is dressed when he should be reacting to the peaceful behavior exhibited by the decoy.

If the dog is not trained in obedience, have the decoy display the same passive behavior while you produce the dog's favorite toy or treat, and see if the dog will leave the non-aggressive decoy to play or receive his favorite reward. A dog that can shift his focus away from the decoy can easily learn neutral reactions, which are very important and will usually result in good impulse control later. This will reduce the number of bad bites you experience and decrease your liability problems in the future. A dog with mental balance also can learn to bite passive suspects when the time comes, so you need not worry about that.

Once you have determined that the dog is not biting things without reason, you can stake him out (back-tie him) to something solid or have a person who is unknown to the dog hold his leash. Have a competent decoy work the dog while you evaluate his potential for the types of aggression you are interested in. See my book *K9 Decoys and Aggression: A Manual for Training Police Dogs* (Brush Education, 2015) for descriptions of the different types of aggression. When you have seen enough to be certain that the dog has high levels of the appropriate types of aggression, have the decoy stop working with and stimulating the dog and wait a few minutes. Then have the decoy approach the dog in a neutral or passive manner, again without displaying any threatening or stimulating signals. A good candidate dog will not show aggression at this point since there is no justification for it and he has had sufficient time to calm down (see Figures 1.1, 1.2, and 1.3).

Figure 1.1 Wearing a bite suit, the decoy approaches the dog in a neutral manner, and the dog remains calm.

Figure 1.2 The decoy stimulates dog, which shows appropriate aggression.

Figure 1.3 The decoy freezes for one minute and re-approaches the dog in a neutral manner. This should be enough time for a clear-headed dog to regain a calm demeanor.

If the dog continues to act aggressively when there is no reason for such behavior, he will likely have control problems later. This doesn't mean you can't train this animal, but it does mean that there is a better dog out there and that it's in your best interest to keep looking for him.

Whether you use the above described method or have your own approach to testing dogs for the presence of a reasonable attitude and a clear head, make sure that this is an important item in your decision to accept or reject a canine candidate. A dog should react aggressively only when the decoy shows bad behavior, not any time the decoy is in a bite suit or sleeve. When bad behavior from the decoy ceases, there is no longer any reason for the dog to be aggressive, and he should calm down in a reasonably short amount of time. Dogs that can do this will easily learn aggression control taught using modern, positive techniques. Dogs that cannot keep a clear head will have difficulty.

> **When bad behavior from the decoy ceases, the dog should calm down in a reasonably short amount of time. Dogs that can do this will easily learn aggression control taught using modern, positive techniques. Dogs that cannot keep a clear head will have difficulty.**

So why do we see so many dogs with unreasonable responses? We see them because we keep paying people money for such animals. When we refuse to pay money for unreasonable dogs, breeders and vendors will stop bringing them to us. The good ones already have. If we keep our standards at a low level and reward providers for showing us difficult animals, such animals will continue to appear. We must stop rewarding the providers economically for bringing us unsuitable dogs. When we do, we will start seeing strong but balanced, clear-headed dogs that are suitable for aggression control training. We control the economic rewards—it is up to us.

The Yerkes-Dodson Law

As stated above, aggression-control work requires dogs to be able to think while they are excited. Many of the imported dogs we have been working with lately are having difficulty with this, so a look at the relationship between excitement and cognitive abilities seems to be in order.

In the early 20th century, psychologists Robert M. Yerkes and John D. Dodson began looking at the relationship between emotional arousal and performance. They published a paper in 1908 in which they described what is now known as the Yerkes-Dodson Law, or the "inverted U." As Figure 1.4 shows, they noticed an optimum level of excitement or arousal for any given task. As excitement levels drop or increase from this optimum, performance decreases.

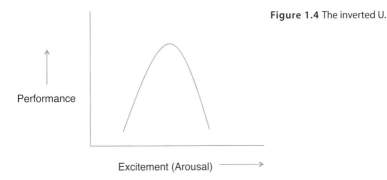

Figure 1.4 The inverted U.

CONSIDER NATURAL EXCITEMENT LEVELS

Dogs that start on the left side of the inverted U need to have their excitement levels increased to reach good performance levels, whereas dogs starting on the right side of the curve need to have their excitement levels decreased to perform well. All our decisions need to be made in light of where we think our dog is on the curve and which way our actions will push him. While there are bound to be minor exceptions to every rule, the Yerkes-Dodson Law has been well accepted for a hundred years now, and we should pay attention to it.

The natural excitement levels of the dog are heavily influenced by genetics and early experience. If we did not personally breed and raise the dog we are training, we have had little influence over his natural excitement levels, but we are still responsible for recognizing animals that are too excitable to make good police dogs. We should learn to recognize dogs whose arousal levels are optimum and those whose levels are too high for good performance.

One of the major differences between police service dogs and sport dogs is that police dogs must think well enough to solve problems even when highly excited and under stress. Their ability to release the adversary and return to cover with only a verbal command from their handlers is critical for their survival when, for example, an ordinary deployment surprisingly turns into a gun battle. More than this, we must never select animals that will be so difficult to control that their handlers will be tempted to break cover in a dangerous situation, simply because their dogs are being difficult. In a tactically difficult situation, there's nothing better than a good dog that thinks well and is controllable, and this is directly linked to the type of dog we select for training in the first place. We must select dogs whose genetics and upbringing place them in the upper left-hand portion of the inverted U so that when excitement levels increase, they will still be capable of good performance.

> **We should learn to recognize dogs whose arousal levels are optimum and those whose levels are too high for good performance. One of the major differences between police service dogs and sport dogs is that police dogs must think well enough to solve problems even when highly excited and under stress.**

What is happening far too often is that we are accepting dogs into training whose genetics and upbringing place them in the upper right-hand part of the curve. Then when the procedures and situations involved in training and deployment increase their excitement levels, these dogs are pushed too far to the right on the curve and their performances suffer terribly. This eventually puts their handlers at risk, all because we made a bad choice about which dogs to take into training. It is time for us to recognize that highly motivated dogs can focus on the task at hand. Any energy the dog cannot focus is simply wild and uncontrollable, not a sign of "high drive." All too often wild, uncontrollable dogs are being confused for highly motivated dogs and are selected for training.

ADJUST YOUR TECHNIQUE TO THE DOG

The training and handling procedures we employ generate characteristic amounts of arousal or excitement. We must be careful to choose techniques that are appropriate for each individual dog. Dogs that start out on the left side of the inverted U will require more excitement from their handlers, whereas those on the right side of the curve will need calm or even dull procedures.

Trainers must constantly adjust their techniques to match the dogs they are training. Years ago, the only dogs that were available for training had medium excitement levels, which placed them somewhere in the middle of the left side of the curve. Consequently, training techniques were developed to increase their excitement levels. With time these techniques became standard and were applied to all dogs indiscriminately. Now that we are training more imported dogs with higher excitement levels, these old techniques are getting us into trouble. We can no longer excite dogs randomly and get away with it. We must develop calmer techniques that keep our high-end dogs in the top part of the curve and maximize their performance. What the future holds cannot be predicted except that as our dogs' gene pool changes, we must make whatever adjustments are necessary to keep them at the proper excitement levels.

We can no longer excite dogs randomly and get away with it. We must develop calmer techniques that keep our high-end dogs in the top part of the curve and maximize their performance.

2

Obedience and Choosing a Method

Obedience Sets the Stage

When done correctly, bite work and aggression control are simply extra phases of obedience. The dog is worked in obedience from location to location, from decoy to decoy, and occasionally the dog is expected to act aggressively and bite, but the sequence is always followed by a return to control since bite work is always done in the middle of an obedience workout. Dogs quickly adjust to this pattern and realize that no matter how exciting and wild aggression work gets, it is always followed by control. They also learn that this is normal, nothing to be avoided or resented.

TRAIN WITH CONSISTENT EXPECTATIONS

The problem for most dogs is that we separate the phases of obedience and bite work during initial training and have different expectations of the dogs for each phase. During obedience, they are required to think in a controlled manner, but during the aggression phase, they are allowed to be as wild as they like, and we do not require them to come back under control. This causes great difficulty for them in real-life situations where there is no separation between phases and they are expected to combine the lessons of obedience and aggression.

The problem for most dogs is that we separate the phases of obedience and bite work during initial training and have different expectations of the dogs for each phase.

This separation of phases in training is a throwback to days when we did not know as much about selecting dogs as we do now. In those days, we selected many weak dogs for training, and hence, we required this controlled–uncontrolled approach, but such is not the case now. The quality of dog that enters training is better today than it has ever been; in fact, as noted in the previous chapter, it is more common to see dogs that are too wildly aggressive than it is to see weak ones. These better animals are quite capable of understanding that obedience and bite work are the same phase of training and that the rules for both are exactly the same. It is usually the human handler who has difficulty understanding this. Time and time again I meet handlers who have dogs with control problems because of the way they handle their dogs. For example, during obedience, if handlers give the Down command, they expect the dogs to down quickly and to assume the correct position and alignment. However, when they give the same command during aggression work, they allow the dogs to down in a slower manner or not at all, and when the dogs finally do, if they are crooked in alignment the handlers say nothing. After all, these handlers reason, the dog is highly excited and distracted, so if she doesn't down, that is understandable; in fact, if she downs at all, that is pretty good. Who cares how she does it?

Well, the dog cares. Dogs are quite capable of learning concepts, and we get so focused on specific actions that many times we fail to pay attention to the concepts we are teaching. When you have different expectations for the Down in obedience than in aggression work, you teach the dog that the rules are different in those two phases. The dog learns that when aggression is involved, she can behave differently than she does in obedience, and her handler will accept that. When you do this, you also teach the dog that whenever she gets excited, it is acceptable for her to behave badly. If all this is true for the Down, the dog will wonder what else it is true for and will begin testing to find out. Unfortunately, most find out that the rules are different for everything. This discovery produces a lot of dogs with control problems.

AVOID PROBLEMS DOWN THE ROAD

How can you avoid these problems? You have to think ahead by planning for aggression control during the very first obedience session. Everything you do should be in preparation for what is to come later. We know the dog eventually will be required to act normally in the presence of a decoy in full gear. She will also be expected to obey obedience commands when she is extremely excited, and, in particular, she will be expected to release things from her mouth when she is extremely excited. You know that in real life there is no separation between bite work and obedience— they exist in the same time frame. You know that when a dog call becomes a gun fight, a dog that can be recalled from a distance and put in a Down under cover has a much higher chance of surviving the situation than a dog that cannot be controlled. Many handlers break cover to gain control of their dogs when they refuse commands during tactical situations. These handlers are unwilling to sacrifice their canine partners and expose themselves to greater risks than they would have to if they had a better controlled dog. Control problems often put handlers at risk, as well as dogs.

BRING THE DECOY TO OBEDIENCE TRAINING

To prepare the dog for these situations, you start with the decoy. There should be a decoy in full protective gear present for most, if not all, obedience sessions. He should not act in an aggressive manner or try to cause trouble for the handlers or their dogs. The dog should become accustomed to working calmly and precisely around the decoy. The emphasis should be on how the decoy is acting, not what he is wearing or carrying. This will help prevent dogs from reacting aggressively at a later stage simply because the decoy appears on the field. The dogs will learn that normal behaviors from the decoy require a normal, non-aggressive response and that the rules for obedience when a decoy is present are exactly the same as when he is not. It is better for the dog to learn this first, instead of allowing uncontrolled, wild behavior around decoys and then trying to punish the dog into controlled behavior later. Good trainers have known for a long time that it is better to teach the acceptable alternative first and then try to eliminate the others than to do it in reverse order. It would make sense to do this in aggression control, too.

AGGRESSION: JUST A FORM OF BEHAVIOR

Let us take a quick break to establish an important fact. Aggression is simply another form of behavior. It is not a mysterious monster that defies the laws of behavioral science. The same laws of learning, reinforcement, and punishment that apply to obedience, agility, article search, tracking, trailing, area search, and detection work apply to aggression as well. You do not have to treat the dog differently simply because you are dealing with aggression. If you can use tools such as praise, games, and toys in the obedience, tracking, and detection phases, you can use them effectively in aggression control as well. Aggression is just another form of behavior.

> Aggression is simply another form of behavior. It is not a mysterious monster that defies the laws of behavioral science. We do not have to treat the dog differently simply because we are dealing with aggression.

TEACH THAT COMPLIANCE = FUN

Once the dog is acting normally around the decoy, you need to define how much freedom she will have in the future. This affects the way the dog will relate to control work later. Teach the dog from the very start that when she complies with obedience commands, life is fun. There is never a good reason to refuse a command, because what she can gain from doing the correct thing is always better than what she will get if she does something else. Teach the dog that it is always in her best interest to do as you say.

This concept does not necessarily need to be taught through pain and force, and how you define the handler in the dog's mind through this process is important. The relationship between dog and handler is a critical factor later when you begin aggression control work. It is much better for all concerned if the handler is always part of the solution instead of part of the problem. Too many trainers and handlers set up the handler as someone who takes things away and is part of the problem the dog must solve instead of as a friend and partner who will help her solve whatever problem the pair are facing. An adversarial relationship between dog and handler works against the team later when the dog must release the decoy and return to the handler's control. Many handlers who have not been established as friendly leaders and partners have great difficulty when their dogs begin to fight them mentally during control work.

An adversarial relationship can begin during obedience training if you constantly use force and pain, teaching dogs that their handlers are not really on their side and that cheating and evading what handlers want is beneficial. Instead, teach dogs that their handlers are always offering what the dogs will enjoy the most, and there is no need to evade the handlers' wishes. Then, when you follow this up with the concept that you will never, ever accept disobedience (keeping after the dog until you get what you want), you have a complete behavioral package that will serve everyone well later. Too many trainers still go straight to pain and force, which results in dogs that cheat and compete later in training and in the field.

Many handlers who have not been established as friendly leaders and partners have great difficulty when their dogs begin to fight them mentally during control work. This unnecessarily adversarial relationship can begin during obedience training.

USE REALISTIC LOCATIONS

Getting back to the idea that there is no separation between obedience and aggression in real life, you should pay some attention to the locations in which you teach obedience. Many times, trainers begin obedience training in an open grassy area that has no resemblance to the areas you need the dog to work in later. This is not an evil thing; these areas are simply available and pleasant for the dog. However, when you set demanding standards on a football field and then lessen your expectations when you move to areas around cars, roads, and buildings, you have again taught the dog that obedience is a separate phase and is of secondary importance. You then end up with dogs that ignore commands when they are in or around their cars and are difficult to control in the very locations where you need control the most. Sound familiar?

Fortunately, this problem can be alleviated by teaching obedience in and around the dog's vehicle from the very start. When training around cars, choose safe parking lots or quiet roads, and make sure each session has the dog jumping in and out of her vehicle and obeying some obedience commands right inside the car. Have the decoy interact in a friendly manner during this time so the dog learns that she must behave properly around vehicles and decoys. This will pay off later when the dog must do aggression control at vehicle stops. Be sure to include buildings (inside and outside) and any other locations you will expect the dog to show control in. In general, teach obedience in the most realistic locations possible right from the start, and you will be in much better shape when you get to aggression control.

INTRODUCE GUNFIRE

Teaching the dog to have a neutral reaction to the decoy's calm presence, as well as his equipment, can be extended to other things that dogs associate with aggression and biting. You can help them retain control by breaking up these associations, teaching neutral responses during obedience. The classic example is the sound of gunfire. Tactical experts are clear in their preference for dogs that do not react to either the sight of a firearm in the hands of the handler or the sound of gunfire. This kind of neutrality can be accomplished easily by firing guns from a distance during obedience training and demanding the same normal performance as always.

> **Teaching the dog to have a neutral reaction to the decoy's calm presence, as well as his equipment, can be extended to other things that dogs associate with aggression and biting. You can help them retain control by breaking up these associations, teaching neutral responses during obedience.**

Some trainers have had good success having the handler produce a toy or reward every time the dog hears gunfire. With time, the dog begins to check in with her handler every time she hears a gun, which gives the handler control over the situation. With time, the gun can be moved closer and closer until the desired proximity is reached. Develop drills in which the handler assumes different defensive positions and draws an empty pistol, aims it, and changes magazines. Be sure to include the prone position in this exercise, since lowering the body is a signal in the dog world to "come here," and many dogs will break whatever position you put them in to come over and see what you are doing when they first see you lie down. The dog needs to hold whatever position you and the handler put her in without interfering with the handler's shooting ability, regardless of what you are doing. Eventually the handler should be able to fire blanks or live rounds at the range without any reaction from the dog. You should not be satisfied until your dogs can do this. At the same time, you can't be excessive with this; dogs have sensitive hearing that can be damaged.

Do not forget whatever formation you will be using for tactical tracking and building searches. Have the formation move as a unit during obedience and teach the dog not to react to the backup officers when they begin firing first. Without this training, most dogs turn on the backups in a real situation and take them out without hesitation. When this has happened a few times, no one wants to go with you on high-risk tracks, and it gets lonely out there. You should be able to do anything you want with firearms and have your dog react in a neutral manner. This will be a great advantage later when the dog must show control after she has heard gunfire.

As stated above, this is an area where toys and games have been used quite effectively. For years, trainers and handlers have used toys to teach a neutral response to gunfire. Introduce the toy during regular obedience training, and continue to employ it as a reward for obedience even when the handler draws a gun and uses all the equipment on his/her belt, and in all positions, including prone. When the dog stays in a calm Down during this, the handler should reward her with a toy or game. Then, from a distance, introduce gunfire from a small-caliber firearm. When the dog looks toward the source of the gunfire, the handler can use a toy to refocus her attention. With time, the dog will begin to anticipate the toy and will look to her handler whenever she hears gunfire. Larger caliber firearms are then fired from a distance and moved closer and closer to the dog until she always remains calm and looks to her handler, even when people are firing right in front of her.

INTRODUCE TACTICAL PROCEDURES
When your dog bites a suspect in real life, and that suspect surrenders, your dog will be commanded to release the person. She will then be expected to follow certain procedures, such as lying

down and guarding the suspect, or returning immediately to her handler, or maybe a combination of both. These procedures should be thoroughly taught during obedience before the dog does bite work, until they are almost second nature to her. If you will later be asking the dog to guard suspects during arrest and handcuffing procedures, it will help to introduce these during obedience training, too.

For example, it is a sound tactical decision for the handler to remain under cover at a distance from the dog and the suspect and control the situation with verbal commands. During training, consider having the suspect face away from the handler and walk backward toward him/her under the watchful eye of the dog, which remains in a Down. As the suspect gets too far away from the dog, the handler should stop the suspect and then call the dog. When the dog reaches the suspect, the handler should ask the dog to down again and then command the suspect to continue backing toward the handler. This process keeps handlers under cover while their dogs are always close enough to prevent the suspects from escaping. Any procedures of this nature, whether tactical leapfrogging with backup officers or building entry with a tactical team, should always first be taught in obedience training.

Certain verbal commands for people are worth including at this point. When you issue a verbal challenge to a person later, you will need to hear what they are saying back to you. You do not need a dog that is barking uncontrollably and keeping you from hearing what is going on. This is particularly true in building searches. For weeks before they are used during aggression work, all challenges and warnings to which you want the dog to respond neutrally should be used in obedience at full volume when there is nothing associated with those words and the dog is expected to pay attention to her obedience. Remember that calmness and excitement are behaviors; they can be rewarded just like anything else.

USE TOYS AND GAMES

Many trainers know the value of using toys and games as rewards during obedience, tracking, and detection work. They have noticed higher levels of performance when they use these motivators. When they have dogs that are suitable for the work, trainers can use toys and games during obedience and still get top performance during aggression work. These dogs can track for toys and still bite adversaries at the end of high-risk tracks and perform as well as ever during aggression work. The dogs can search intensely for their toys during the detection phases and still show their usual enthusiasm for aggression work.

PROOFING AGAINST TOYS

This approach, however, has not been without controversy. When civilian obedience trainers first began using toys and games to improve performance, there was concern that the dogs involved would break obedience when they encountered children playing with the dog's favorite toy on the street. The trainers discovered that dogs had individual reactions to this temptation but that all sound dogs could be trained to ignore toys the same way that food-reward dogs are trained to ignore hot dogs dropped in the park by children. Stray hot dogs and toys are simply distractions that can be trained against. This training became known as "proofing" the dog against food or toys. This approach has been so successful that trainers currently have no doubts about the practical efficiency of using toys during obedience training, provided the dogs are properly "proofed" against the toys as part of the process. Their dogs are completely reliable in the real world.

When tracking trainers began to use toys as the reward at the end of the track and even as multiple rewards left along the track, there was concern that the dogs would only be looking for toys at the end of their tracks and would not engage an adversary should the need arise. What these trainers discovered was that if an adversary was occasionally placed at the end of a track, dogs that already enjoyed aggression work were more than willing to ignore toys on the track to engage a human. It has become clear that dogs that are suitable for the work will work hard to obtain toys and games but can be effectively "proofed" against the distraction of toys and games when the handler says it is time to work. It has also become clear that suitable dogs will choose toys and games when they are the only rewards available, but they will choose the excitement of a good fight over a toy or a treat whenever possible. In general, toys and games have increased many dogs' motivational levels in different phases of training and have not interfered with the aggressive potential of dogs that are suitable for the work and have good trainers who know how to balance them properly. Again, aggression is simply a behavior. It does not defy the laws of science, and we do not have to treat our dogs differently in later phases simply because we are dealing with aggression.

> **In general, toys and games have increased many dogs' motivational levels in different phases of training and have not interfered with the aggressive potential of dogs that are suitable for the work and have good trainers.**

TEACH CONTROLED EXCITEMENT

An interesting use of obedience to prepare a dog for aggression control is to teach her to release a toy before you ask her to release anything else (like a decoy) later, when she is more excited. It is not clear when this technique was first used, but it has been around for a very long time. It has several advantages worth considering. This method allows the handler to introduce excitement gradually (proper game playing is a form of excitement), never increasing it quite enough to make the dog lose control but building the dog's tolerance for excitement with each training session. During this process, the dog is always required to come back under control and the rules of obedience remain the same even when the dog is getting more and more excited.

This technique allows us to teach excitement under control, independently of aggression and bite work, so that if problems arise, we can work on them without having any direct effect on the quality of the dog's aggression. The dog soon learns that releasing things from her mouth is simply a normal part of obedience, the rules of which never change. She knows that, as with everything else in obedience, her handler and her trainer will never accept disobedience or sloppy behavior, regardless of the location or circumstances (remember that you are doing obedience around decoys in full equipment, around cars, and in locations where you will do tactical work later). And there is no need to evade the command since good things that the dog will enjoy always follow the procedure.

MAKE THE HANDLER PART OF THE SOLUTION

This is a good time to teach another concept, namely that when the handler tells the dog to release something from her mouth, the handler is not an adversary who is merely taking something away. The handler will give the object back quickly, will provide another toy that is just as much fun, or will find a way to change the game into something else that is almost as much fun as the original. The handler will make sure that the dog never has to give up what is in her mouth for nothing. The handler is on the dog's side. In the dog's mind, her handler is part of the solution, not part of the problem. This cooperative relationship helps reduce the problem of dogs cheating and evading commands later when you ask them to release the most exciting thing of all, a human being. What she will get for releasing the human may not be quite as exciting as the fight itself, but it will be a close second. The dog will know she will never be asked to give up something for nothing, or merely to avoid pain. When her handler is involved, disobedience or sloppiness will never be accepted, but there will always be something in it for the dog. Animals that think this way are much easier to work with in aggression control.

The handler will ensure that the dog never has to give up what is in her mouth for nothing. The handler is on the dog's side. In the dog's mind, her handler is part of the solution, not part of the problem. This cooperative relationship helps reduce the problem of dogs cheating and evading commands later when you ask them to release the most exciting thing of all, a human being.

ONLY THE HANDLER GIVES TOYS

Obedience is not considered complete until the dog is "proofed" of all toys and games to the point that when she is working she is not tempted to accept them from anyone but her handler. If you are not experienced in this, a good obedience trainer can help. If proofing is not complete, there will be trouble later when these items are used for reinforcement of good behavior. If proofing is not maintained, you will also have trouble. To reduce the need for pain compliance, you must incorporate a complete system of training wherein the dog is always prepared for what comes next. If you begin preparing her during obedience for the use of toys and games later, you will increase the quality of the dog's life immeasurably, and training will be smooth and pleasurable for both dog and human. If you take shortcuts or fail to maintain proofing, you will get all the trouble you can imagine.

Choosing a Method

Once you have selected a suitable dog (see Chapter 1) and obedience is working properly for you, it is necessary to select a method for teaching the dog to release the decoy. Trainers will probably always have individual approaches to this as they have with everything else. What is important is that each trainer choose a method that makes sense to them so that they will put their heart and soul into their efforts and remain committed without quitting in the middle of the process. It is also important to choose a method that teaches the dog that the handler is on the dog's side and is not one more limitation that the dog must defeat to get what she wants. Dogs that see the handler as a supporter who is there to help them tend to fight harder for us and learn aggression control much more easily than others. They also have less need or desire to cheat on us or evade our wishes later, since they understand that we are not there just to take things away from them but are there to help.

Table 2.1 is an attempt to steer trainers to the sections of this book that describe methods that will suit their individual preferences while still maintaining a good bond between dog and handler.

Table 2.1 Training Alternatives

Trainer's preference	Refer to	Chapter
To have dog indicate without biting	Sit and Bark	3 (p. 27)
	Re-find	3 (p. 30)
To avoid using toys or games	Self Out	4 (p. 34)
	Muzzle	5 (p. 49)
To avoid dropping sleeve	Self Out	4 (p. 34)
	Muzzle	5 (p. 49)
	Toys and Games	6 (p. 57)
To utilize sleeve dropping	Sleeve Transfer	6 (p. 67)
To maximize use of toys and games	Toys and Games	6 (p. 57)
	Self Out with Toys	4 (p. 41)
	Sleeve Transfer	6 (p. 67)
	Muzzle with Games	5 (p. 50)

3

Indicating without Biting

Many trainers wish to control aggression in their dogs by not using aggression at all. This is particularly prevalent in the search-and-rescue community, but even a few law-enforcement agencies prefer to limit their liability by using dogs that indicate a person's location without biting them. There are several approaches to training a dog to indicate without biting. If you don't already have a favorite method, two of the more common approaches are described in this chapter.

Preparation

As with many important skills, the foundations for a good Sit and Bark are established in obedience. Those of you who skipped Chapter 2 should go back and read it now. Be sure you also understand the principle of modular training, and specifically back chaining as described below.

BACK CHAINING

Practitioners of modular training cite the advantages of breaking complex behaviors down into small components and teaching each separately. In back chaining, a complex behavior is broken down into individual components much like the links in a chain.

Each component is taught separately, and when all have been learned properly, they are put together much as one would connect the links in a chain. Any problems are diagnosed and dealt with individually as part of a particular link. What is interesting about back chaining is that it works most effectively if the links are put together in reverse chronological order. We identify the behavior that comes last in the sequence and teach it first. Then we teach the second to last, then the third to last, and so on, working backward until we finally teach the first behavior and connect them all, like links in a chain.

Practitioners of this technique frequently mention the advantages of breaking complex behaviors down into small components and teaching each separately.

In this way, no matter what is being taught, the dog always knows what comes next and knows how to succeed in the next task, so he is never running ahead into the unknown (which makes him insecure). Instead he is constantly proceeding to a task at which he already knows how to succeed, which minimizes confusion. This builds the dog's self-confidence and his trust in the handler as someone who's never confusing and with whom he always succeeds. In addition to improving the relationship between the handler and the dog, back chaining seems to increase the speed of learning and how long the dog remembers complex sets of behaviors. Whether you call it modular training or back chaining, it is a concept worth keeping in mind.

When you use back chaining, you ensure that the dog always knows how to handle what comes next and that he remains confident in his ability to succeed.

Teaching the Sit and Bark

The last thing a dog must do when indicating the position of a human is to sit and bark, so this is what you should teach first. One way to do this is to hold the dog's favorite toy or treat above your head while facing the dog at close range, as in Figure 3.1. Encouraging the dog to look up like this usually raises his head, while his rear end often goes in the opposite direction. This encourages him to sit. When he sits, immediately mark that behavior and reward him. Teasing the dog when he is in the Sit by delaying delivery of the reward and stimulating him with the toy or treat will usually prompt the dog to make some kind of sound, which the handler should, again, mark and reward. Be careful not to overstimulate dogs that are obsessed with toys as they will sometimes bite you to get one.

As soon as the dog is sitting and barking reliably, work on any changes you would like to see in the dog's positioning. This can be done easily by adjusting where the reward is delivered. If he is not sitting close enough to the person he is to indicate, throw the reward directly in front of the subject's feet so the dog must close the distance to get it, as in Figure 3.2. When this is done many times in a row, the dog will begin to "cheat" by sitting closer to the human subject to get the reward faster, and that is exactly what you want. If the dog is sitting at the desired distance, throw the reward directly to him.

> As soon as the dog is sitting and barking reliably, work on any changes you would like to see in the dog's positioning. This can be done easily by adjusting where the reward is delivered.

If he is sitting too close to the human subject, throw the reward high in the air so it lands far behind him, making him turn around and chase it, as in Figure 3.3. When this is done enough times for the dog to expect that the reward will always be thrown

Figure 3.1 Teaching the last thing first. Decoy Bill Nott holds the dog's toy above his head at close range, which encourages the dog to sit. Teasing with the toy will encourage the dog to bark.

Figure 3.2 The toy is thrown in front of the dog, encouraging him to move forward to get it. Use this technique to adjust the dog's position to closer to the decoy.

behind him, he will begin to "cheat" by sitting back farther from the human subject and preparing to intercept the reward going over his head. That is, of course, exactly what you want him to do.

Once the dog is reliably sitting and barking at the correct distance, the human subject should change positions (standing, sitting, prone, and so forth) so that the dog will perform well regardless of how the subject appears or what he or she is doing (see Figure 3.4). If you wish the dog to be scent specific, this is the time to begin working on that so the dog masters everything you expect of him when he finds someone, but masters it at short range before he ever begins searching. If you start the dog searching without this foundation, he will not know what to do when he makes contact with the human subject. He will be excited by the running and searching and will have more difficulty learning the entire sequence of behaviors you expect of him. If you teach the sequence using back chaining, as described above, it makes it much easier on the dog.

If the dog does not continue going to source when he begins searching, there are three major possibilities. One, you have rushed too fast through the short-range training; two, the dog doesn't really like the reward you are offering enough to work hard for it; or three, he doesn't think the reward is at the source because the handler has been carrying and giving it. Fortunately, there are simple solutions for all three problems. In the first case, return to the basics at short range and go slower this time. In the second, do some preference tests to determine what reward the dog wants to work for. In the third, put the reward with the human subject so the dog always expects to find it there and have the handler give it only occasionally.

When the dog is performing well at close range, he is allowed to start farther away from the human subject so that he approaches from a short distance. If the foundation is set well, this will present no problems since the dog already knows what to do when he reaches the human. With time, start the dog farther and farther

Figure 3.3 The toy is thrown high over the dog's head to land behind him, encouraging the dog to move backward or turn around to get it. This technique helps adjust the dog's position to farther away from the decoy.

Figure 3.4 Decoy kneeling. Next comes sitting, lying prone, facing away from the dog, and so on. You want the dog to perform well no matter what the subject is doing.

away from the human subject, until he is doing short searches followed by longer and longer searches.

Many trainers teaching the Bark and Hold—where the dog sits, barks, and bites the human if he tries to escape—have found this training approach useful to teach the initial search behaviors. Then, later in the process, they switch the dog over to biting the escaping human. Good dogs that are well-suited to aggression work have no trouble switching from toys to biting and have performed well on the street.

> **Many trainers teaching the Bark and Hold have found this training approach useful to teach the initial search behaviors. Then, later in the process, they switch the dog over to biting the escaping human.**

The Re-find

Some trainers wish to produce a dog that will range away from the handler until he finds a person, return to the handler to give a special signal indicating he has found someone, and then bring the handler back to the subject he has located. Often referred to as the Re-find, this procedure is also best taught using back chaining:

- First, teach the dog to bring the handler to the subject.
- Then teach the dog to return to the handler who is approaching too slowly.
- Next teach the dog to give a special signal after returning before bringing the handler to the subject.
- Last, teach the dog to find the subject before coming back to the handler, giving the special signal, and taking the handler to the subject.

In this manner, the dog always knows what to do next and does not get confused.

Figure 3.5 The ceremony of passing the reward from the subject (on the reader's left) to the handler (on the right), while the dog pays close attention.

Again, drills should start at very short range with no searching involved. The dog is allowed to move a step or two toward the subject who has the reward. It is important that the subject always has the reward so that the dog always has a reason to go to source. It is also important that the subject never gives the reward to the dog but waits until the handler arrives (which should be quickly) and makes a ceremony of passing the reward to the handler, who then gives the reward, as in Figure 3.5. The dog learns that the reward is always with the subject but the subject will never give it to him. On the other hand, the handler would give it to him but the handler never has it. Good dogs are not stupid; they quickly learn that the only way they are going to get the reward is to get these two people together.

> **The dog learns that the reward is always with the subject but the subject will not give it to him. The handler would give it to him but the handler never has it. Good dogs are not stupid; they quickly learn that the only way they are going to get the reward is to get these two people together.**

INCREASE THE DISTANCE

Next, you need to increase the distance slightly so that the handler can start coming more and more slowly. If the dog really wants the reward, he will be frustrated and start coming back for the handler, trying to get his handler to hurry up, as in Figure 3.6. Now we have the dog going to the subject and returning for the handler, but all at fairly short range with no searching. The next thing to do is teach the dog to give the special signal, as in Figure 3.7, before you approach the subject. Some handlers like to have the dog jump up on them; some prefer to have the dog bump their hand with his nose; some have the dog bump or bite a toggle on the handler's belt; others have the dog sit or down in front of the handler. The signal can be as individual as necessary, as long as the dog is willing to give it and the handler can read it.

Figure 3.6 When the handler is too slow, the dog comes back to encourage him to hurry up.

Figure 3.7 After going to the decoy and returning, the dog gives the special signal to get the handler to come with him. In this case, the signal is to turn away from the handler and perform a Down.

Now that the dog is the master of what to do when he finds his human subject, you can start doing runaways and hiding the subject from view without confusing the dog about what comes next. At this point, adding a beginning search command and the words "Show me" after the special signal, would be nice. Soon the dog will be doing short searches followed by longer and longer ones with no difficulty, performing a strong Re-find every time.

4

The Self Out

Originally called the Combined Method, the Self Out does not require any toys or game playing to be effective. Trainers who are worried about their dogs looking for toys instead of concentrating on the adversary can use this method and their dogs will never even see a toy.

Preparation for this technique includes everything discussed in Chapter 2 on obedience, so all of you who skipped the second chapter, go back and read it now before you go any further. Chapter 2 was not written so that you could skip it. It was written because the material in it directly affects the teaching of control during aggression work. Obedience really does set the stage.

The Self Out relies on muscle physiology and the trainer's ability to read the dog. Muscles produce lactic acid, or lactate, when they contract. When the lactic acid reaches a certain concentration, muscles get sore, experience fatigue, and eventually stop working. This is a physiological fact and cannot be changed. The muscles in the dog's jaw are subject to this just like any other muscle. So, no matter how tough the dog, if she must bite hard to hold on to something, she will eventually fatigue chemically and be forced to release the object. Dogs do not seem to enjoy this experience any more than human athletes enjoy fatigue and exhaustion. When they have suffered through it a few times, they seek ways to avoid it. So this technique involves working the dog as we normally would to get her to bite and then keeping her on the bite for as long as she can physically hold on. When you work on the bite itself, you calm down and say nothing or you gently encourage the dog since she is doing exactly what you told her to do. You simply wait for the fatigue to set in, at which time the dog will release by herself. We allow the aggression to extinguish. During the fatigue phase, the quality of the bite may suffer, but this is only due to the fatigue and does not cause problems with the bite later.

As the dog releases on her own, speak the release command (hopefully already taught to the dog for releasing her favorite toy during obedience, see Chapter 2) and tell the dog what a good dog she is. Because of this process, you will have a dog that wants to bite, but after a short period of biting is motivated to avoid the long road to fatigue. In other words, you have a dog that initially wants to bite but after a short time actually wants to release. All you have to do is to hold off on the release command until the dog is going to release anyway, and you are guaranteed compliance with no resistance from the dog and without the necessity for harsh treatment. When this is done repeatedly, the dog associates the command with the action and, eventually, if you can read when the dog is about to release on her own, you can precede the action with the command and your dog will soon be releasing on command. When done correctly, the dog begins to release sooner and sooner, probably due to the desire to avoid the fatigue. Soon she is releasing on command in a normal time frame.

It is important to believe this, because some dogs hold on a very long time in the beginning of the process. Many trainers lose patience and stop using the technique, thinking it doesn't work. It will work if you believe in it, have enough patience, and can read the dog properly. This method has the major advantage of allowing you to teach by rewarding good behavior instead of punishing bad behavior. It has long been known that punishment is only a temporary tool and that what is learned through it must be retaught in a short amount of time. That is why dogs taught through punishment need to be "cleaned up" on a regular basis, often at short time intervals. However, many really tough dogs are also quite smart and learn quickly with positive reinforcement. Handlers using the Self Out simply wait for the dog to do what they want, give the command at the same time, and praise the dog for complying when she was going to do it anyway. The dog can please the handler and avoid reaching fatigue at the same time.

This method has the major advantage of allowing you to teach by rewarding good behavior instead of punishing bad behavior.

The handler is not taking away anything that the dog still wants, so with this procedure no competition develops between dog and handler. Not only do you get the behavior you want, but you also maintain the good relationship between you and the dog. The handler is helping the dog avoid the bad alternative (fatigue), so there is no reason for the dog to resent anything or cheat on her handler. Since the dog will always release eventually, you are free to work on anything else you choose. The quality of the bite can be emphasized during the same time frame as the release. Fullness and power can be developed with every bite, and the dog will still release. The bite will get better and better even as the release improves, and you can begin working on the release as soon as you begin working on the bite. Compared to other techniques, this method increases the number of repetitions you get on the release during the same amount of time. More repetitions are usually a good thing.

> The handler is not taking away anything the dog still
> wants, so with this procedure no competition develops
> between dog and handler. Not only do you get the
> behavior you want, but you also maintain a good
> relationship between you and your dog.

These advantages make the Self Out a good choice for green dogs, and, in fact, it works best with inexperienced dogs that have no bad memories of aggression control work. In the dog's mind the release becomes a natural part of every bite, so it does not become a big issue or point of resistance with her handler.

Counteracting Bad Behavior

While the Self Out is at its best with green, untrained dogs, it is also very effective with experienced animals that have developed bad behaviors. For instance, some dogs are so tough that they can refuse to release the decoy even under the most severe punishments. The more severe the punishment, the more they scream and hang on, biting even harder in most cases. These are cases where the Self Out can help.

Some of these dogs have a genetic predisposition to what is known as pain-induced aggression. These dogs react to pain aggressively, and the more pain they feel, the higher their aggression levels become. When trainers use physical pain on them in the form of punishments, all they do is guarantee that the dogs' aggression levels will increase and that they will bite even harder than before. This prevents the dogs from releasing, even if they want to. The Self Out avoids this complication completely since it does not require the use of punishment or pain.

Other dogs have a genetic predisposition for what is known as redirected aggression. This affects the direction in which the aggression will be expressed. When a trainer or handler punishes such a dog for not releasing, the dog would like to bite her handler for interfering, but the rules of the dog world say they cannot express aggression toward an upper-ranking member of the pack. She knows she can only show serious aggression to lower-ranking pack members. All the aggression the dog would like to use to compete with her handler is thus redirected from the upper-ranking handler to the only lower-ranking animal available—the decoy. The result: again, the dog will bite harder instead of releasing. The Self Out avoids all this by not using punishment.

HANDLER-DOG COMPETITION

Dogs that have learned to compete with their handler and dogs that feel they are dominant over their handler often refuse to release because they don't want to give anything up to their handler. Using the Self Out, the handler only encourages the dog to bite, never trying to take anything away from the dog, so there is nothing for the two of them to fight about.

Through the Self Out, the dominant dog learns she cannot control the situation and run the show like she used to. At the beginning of the bite, the dog feels like she is in control and can have her way. If you keep her on the bite longer than she likes and, in fact, keep her biting to the point of agony, it is clear to the dog that she has lost control, that the humans are in charge, and that there is a good reason to comply with what they want. This is a good concept for dominant dogs to learn, and when they do life gets much better for us in many ways. So, in the beginning, it is important to keep the dog biting to the point of agony with every bite, until she believes the handler will expect this every time. Then when the dog releases faster to avoid the agony, she feels she has beaten the system, which provides an intrinsic, or internal, reward that the handler or trainer cannot, since the dog gives it to herself. One of the problems trainers and handlers have when employing the Self Out is that they allow the dog to release when she is merely tired out instead of taking her to the point of agony with every bite. When they do this, they lose the advantage described above.

OVEREXCITED DOGS

Some dogs cannot handle excitement well. For some, this is a temporary stage they go through and they eventually work out of it, while others are like this throughout their entire careers, which limits their usefulness in many circumstances. For these dogs, the bite alone is so stimulating that anything else, such as punishment or game playing, pushes them over the edge mentally and they refuse to release. They are usually too excited to think clearly and end up on the far right-hand side of the inverted U (see Chapter 1 on the Yerkes-Dodson Law). The Self Out allows the handler and decoy to quietly calm the dog and keep the excitement levels at a minimum. This allows the dog to remain clear in her thinking, which often results in a good release that can be rewarded. Many times, such dogs learn to handle more excitement as they mature and the good release remains.

> The Self Out allows the handler and decoy to quietly calm the dog and keep the excitement levels to a minimum. This allows the dog to remain clear in her thinking, which often results in a good release that can then be rewarded. Many times, the dog learns to handle more excitement as she matures, and the good release remains.

CORRECTING FAULTY TRAINING

Some dogs become frantic on the bite due to the misuse of compulsive techniques by past trainers. They get tense as the handlers approach, even trying to spin the decoys to get away from the punishment they are certain is coming. In such a dog's mind, her handler is part of the problem and needs to be avoided. The Self Out allows you to let the handler stand back and not stress the dog while the release gets better and better. It often improves the relationship between the handler and dog as well.

PAIN IS NOT THE BEST TOOL

Trainers are seeing more and more dogs with extremely high pain thresholds these days. The compulsive techniques developed in the past were effective on animals with average pain thresholds but are proving to be less effective on many of the dogs you see now. The compulsive techniques were based on what behaviorists call an "escape reaction." This is a response to an overwhelming stimulus. This stimulus is so severe that the animal feels she must stop whatever she is doing and try to escape from it. The old techniques relied on the fact that when a dog refused to release, an extremely painful punishment would cause the dog to stop whatever she was doing (in this case biting) to escape from the pain. This resulted in the dog releasing.

It was effective because most dogs had regular or low pain thresholds. These techniques are not working on many of today's dogs because the dogs' pain tolerances are so high (meaning they can tolerate so much pain) that it is difficult to apply enough pain to create an escape reaction. This forces trainers to use what many people feel are abusive techniques in desperate attempts to gain control. These attempts are not only difficult, they are also unnecessary. The Self Out does not require an escape reaction. It therefore is independent of an animal's pain threshold and can be adapted to work well on all dogs. It doesn't need pain to be effective.

Extinction Burst

The extinction burst is an interesting phenomenon involved with using the Self Out. When the decoy stops rewarding the dog with fighting and movement, the dog's aggression begins to decrease.

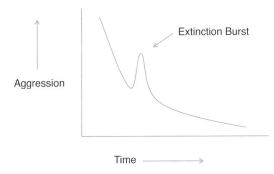

Figure 4.1 An extinction burst is often seen when using the Self Out.

Allowing a behavior to decrease and disappear like this is often referred to as the "extinction" of a behavior. Whenever extinction is used as a behavioral tool, we expect to see what is known as an "extinction burst." The behavior, which has been waning for some time, spikes again and becomes strong, as if there has been no decline (see Figure 4.1). This is a temporary change and if the extinction is continued, the behavior will decline again, continue its downward trend, and disappear. The problem is that trainers who don't understand extinction bursts get discouraged when they see the behavior "returning" and think that the technique is not working. Many give up at this point, thinking that they have wasted their time, when in fact extinction bursts are normal and expected. In fact, they are a sign that the extinction process is working.

> **Allowing a behavior to decrease and disappear like this is often referred to as the "extinction" of a behavior. Whenever extinction is used as a behavioral tool, we expect to see what is known as an "extinction burst."**

Flexibility

Flexibility is another advantage of the Self Out. Trainers who wish to avoid toys and game playing can do so and still get good releases without relying on punishment. Trainers who wish to maximize the reward give the dog a second bite (avoiding the use of toys) or wait until the dog releases and then introduce her favorite toy, which encourages the dog to release sooner and significantly cuts down the overall training time. I first experimented with toys in the early 1980s in an attempt to save decoys' backs when dogs held on for a long time. I then discovered that most dogs respond well to the toys without the Self Out first, which has become a more popular approach (see Chapter 6). Sleeve drops (having the decoy deliberately let go of the sleeve, see Chapter 6) can be used, although the Self Out was originally developed for styles that avoid the sleeve drop. It works well either way (waiting for the dog to release a dropped sleeve is another form of self out). Any style of bite building can be used with the Self Out. It works well on external sleeves (see Figure 4.2), hidden sleeves, muzzles, bite suits, and on prone suspects (see Figures 4.3, 4.4, and 4.5).

Figure 4.2 The author's students using the Self Out with an external sleeve, summer 1981.

Figure 4.3 Dog takes a good bite.

Figure 4.4 Decoy goes prone and handler immediately moves in to protect his head. Dog is allowed to continue biting.

Figure 4.5 When she has fatigued, the dog releases by herself. Note the calm attitude and lack of competition between dog and handler.

Benefits for the Decoy

Although I originated and pioneered the Self Out, a nice adaptation of it is that used by Franco Angelini, who quickly realized that having the decoy lie prone is a good way to reduce the significant strain on his back. It also increases the reward for the dog. If the dog has been working in social aggression (what some trainers incorrectly refer to as the "fight drive"), the reward for this behavior is to see submission in the opponent. The biological function of social aggression is to create and maintain social hierarchies, or pecking orders. A dog that is operating in this type of aggression is fighting to see these signals of submission in her opponent and feels rewarded when she does.

Experienced decoys have long known that one of the ways to reward social aggression is to suddenly start working the dog in predatory aggression since the signals that trigger predatory aggression also signal the submission the dog was fighting to get when she was in social aggression. To put this more simply, having the decoy fall down does two things at the same time: it rewards social aggression (the "fight drive") and both stimulates and rewards predatory aggression (the "prey drive"). So, whatever type of aggression you have been working the dog in, having the decoy lie prone at the end of the bite rewards the dog. The dog feels satisfied, having fulfilled the purpose of the aggression, and is more willing to give up the decoy. Consequently, having the decoy lie prone after the dog bites well is a good way to reward social and predatory aggression. This makes using the Self Out on a prone decoy very useful in several situations (see Figures 4.6, 4.7, 4.8, and 4.9). Creative trainers will find many ways to combine it with their favorite routines.

Figure 4.6 Prone decoy on a front bite.

Figure 4.7 Dog noticing the handler.

Figure 4.8 Relaxed dog receiving praise from the handler after the release.

Figure 4.9 The Self Out can improve the relationship between the dog and handler. The dog has no need to cheat on or compete with the handler.

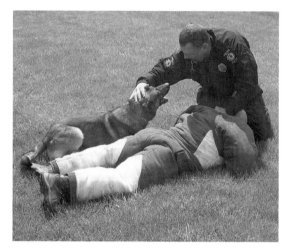

Role of Punishment

The Self Out also offers flexibility regarding punishment, as described earlier. If the Self Out does not rely on punishment, does that mean you must never use it when training the Self Out? No. No method will ever be perfect for all dogs without adjustment. Animals are all unique, and we need to adjust to their different personalities if we are to train them well. While the Self Out can be adjusted to suit any dog, there are a small number of dogs that learn the release well and then just stop doing it. At this point, when you have taught in a positive manner and are sure that the dog understands how to do it correctly, you may have to apply a reasonable punishment. When this is done in a reasonable manner, the dog returns to her former performance level and the relationship between the handler and dog is unharmed. Therefore, the technique was originally called the Combined Method. It allows us to teach with inducive methods, occasionally combined with punishment. If you have taught the release correctly, you won't have to use punishment often, and the severity of the punishment will be much less than if you had used compulsive methods. Looking at its efficiency with different types of dogs and the variety of choices the method gives the trainer, the Self Out is a valuable tool that is well worth using.

CASE EXAMPLE: MAX

Max (not his real name) was a young male German shepherd dog who had worked for a large, inner-city K9 unit for several years before his handler brought him to a state-wide training workshop. He had numerous solid street bites to his credit and had a reputation for being a good dog to have around in a dangerous situation. When it came time to work on aggression control, his handler announced that he really only had one problem: Max had never released a decoy voluntarily, even in basic school. They had tried pinch collars, double pinch collars, sharpened pinch collars, and even electricity with no success; when Max realized there was a correction coming, he would stiffen his neck, scream, and bite harder no matter what happened. He would spin the decoy around to evade his handler whenever possible and would cheat and compete with his handler whenever possible to avoid having to release.

When questioned about Max's other problems, the handler described a very compliant, reasonable dog that was apparently easy to work with in everything else except aggression control. Max performed well in obedience, tracked well, did article search, building search, area search, and everything else he was asked to do well; he simply would not release the bad guy voluntarily.

The handler had adapted his handling style to this and resigned himself to the fact that his dog would never out. This is an important pattern to watch for; bad dogs, or dogs that are unsuitable for the work, are bad at several things, not just the Out. If a dog is suitable for the work, and does everything else well, she will certainly release the decoy if we set it up properly and use appropriate techniques. When a dog performs well at everything else and is only a problem when it is time to out, we are doing something wrong and the situation can be improved. Max seemed to be a classic example of this, and we decided to try the Self Out to see if it would help.

As expected, Max hit hard and bit well on the first bite, holding on a long time before he decided to release. If memory serves, it was a full 25 minutes before Max released that first bite, but at the end he was tired and his jaw muscles were fatigued. He was immediately sent back to bite again, which he did. He only held on for about 10 minutes the second time and only for five minutes on the third bite. After a short break to catch his breath and cool down, he got another set of three bites, and the time he was willing to hold on got shorter and shorter.

Throughout the process, the handler continued to praise Max for biting and for releasing, so the dog understood that both things were good. Soon

Max was not interested in hanging on to decoys at all (his jaws were too fatigued), and his handler started giving the Out command just before Max would have released anyway. When the dog released, the handler gave him maximum praise, and Max, who had never really wanted to be a problem, began to learn that releasing the decoy was actually to his benefit and was another way to please his handler while still getting to bite things.

It doesn't always work this fast, but in a few hours Max was outing normally. The Self Out allowed us to reward good behavior without needing to use punishment, which Max had always fought against. It took away the need for Max to compete with his handler and ushered in a new era of cooperation, forever changing their relationship.

5

The Muzzle

One of the big problems in teaching aggression control comes when the dog already has his teeth in the decoy and refuses to release. Another is when the dog is tempted to cheat just a little bit to get his teeth into the decoy. Most of our problems teaching the Out center on the dog getting his teeth into the decoy or already having his teeth in him. If we remove the dog's teeth from the picture, we take away his major tool for resisting and cheating on us. This is exactly what the muzzle does. It allows us to teach without the fear of the dog latching on to the decoy and disrupting training by holding on for the next 10 or 20 minutes. A good general rule in dog training is that when the teeth are part of the problem, the muzzle may be part of the solution.

A good general rule in dog training is that when the teeth are part of the problem, the muzzle may be part of the solution.

Preparation Is Key

Proper preparation is essential for any type of muzzle work. Go back and read Chapter 2 again and do all the exercises described there with the dog in muzzle. Remember that it is not sufficient for the dog to merely accept the muzzle, the dog must also be so comfortable with it that he focuses through it mentally and almost forgets about it. The dog's mind must be on the environment and what he is doing, not on the muzzle. If he cannot play games like soccer with you without trying to get the muzzle off, he is not ready yet. Keep working until the dog will do perfect obedience and play any game you like without paying any attention to the muzzle.

> **The dog's mind must be on the environment and what he is doing, not on the muzzle. If he cannot play games like soccer with you without trying to get the muzzle off, he is not ready yet.**

Basic Muzzle Exercise

The drawback to this technique is that it must be used in conjunction with a good muzzle attack to be most effective. You therefore need a decoy who is skilled in muzzle work, and not all decoys are. Once you have such a decoy, you simply end each attack with the release command (which should have been taught on toys without the muzzle during non-muzzle obedience sessions, see Chapter 2). If the dog does not cease fighting, you step in and gently yet firmly pull the dog off and place him in whatever position you want him to assume after releasing (usually a Down or a Sit). When he stops fighting you, praise and reward him. The reward can be anything you can physically arrange, including games and toys (if the dog can play with the muzzle on) or if you can remove the muzzle very quickly. It's best to keep the dog on leash if you remove the muzzle, since you don't want the dog to be free enough to run back to the decoy and bite him. For this reason, most people keep the muzzle on and simply praise the dog and make a big fuss over him as a reward. However, that does not mean you can't be creative and play the dog's favorite game from muzzle obedience or something else the dog would enjoy. There is good flexibility here to adjust the technique to suit different philosophies and techniques.

Several repetitions of this sort of exercise give even the toughest dogs a chance to learn what is expected of them. If it is done well, most dogs will comply willingly since there is no pain-induced aggression created by painful punishments to make it difficult for the dog to comply. There is also no chance of that aggression being redirected at the decoy. The handler is helping the dog succeed; no competition or resentment develops if the rewards are sufficient in the dog's mind. Care must be taken with dogs that have excitability problems. Few things in a dog's life are as exciting as a good muzzle workout, so the decoy must be almost boring to control excitement levels in high-end dogs, but at least when such dogs have difficulties, they cannot latch on to the decoy and hang on for long periods.

A dog that has suffered severe punishments with a previous trainer may be tense at first when a new handler first approaches, and he may still try to cheat by moving around the decoy to get away from the handler. However, the dog cannot delay training by hanging onto the decoy with his teeth, and this allows the handler to gently remove and reward the dog for whatever good behavior he exhibits. With time the dog learns that things are different with this handler and that he need not fear the handler's approach. The cheating and competition should begin to decrease at this point. Cheating dogs can still present a problem, though. It is very clear to them when the muzzle is on and when it is off. Some dogs behave perfectly when the muzzle is on because they know there is no chance of getting a bite, but they cheat when the muzzle is off. This does not usually happen when the dog is properly trained in muzzle from the start, but an experienced dog that has already learned to cheat can be difficult to work with and may take many repetitions to work through the problem. Dogs with high pain thresholds have no complications with this approach (since it does not rely on pain) and usually learn well in muzzle.

Sleeve-Happy Dogs

The muzzle can be used by itself or in conjunction with other protective equipment. Some dogs refuse to release anything at any time, and certainly the muzzle is beneficial for them; but it is also useful for dogs that simply have too much focus on the sleeve or the bite suit. These "sleeve-happy" dogs often release with no problem in real situations on the street but are so stimulated by the sight of equipment in training that they refuse to comply when the decoy is wearing equipment of any kind. It can be very difficult to get such dogs certified, since most certification tests require the dog to release a decoy wearing protective equipment. If the decoy sheds equipment, some of these dogs will ignore the decoy and pick up the equipment and thrash it.

Usually such dogs have not been set up properly for aggression control during the obedience phase, as described in Chapter 2, so this needs to be examined, but the muzzle is also useful. Working a sleeve-happy dog in a muzzle when the decoy is fully suited offers trainers and handlers a chance to reward good behavior without having to punish bad behavior. Since the muzzle prevents the dog from behaving badly by hanging on with his teeth, it is easier to help him do the correct thing and gain his reward, even when the decoy is wearing tempting equipment. And gaining that reward for correct behavior eventually leads to better performance (see Figures 5.1 and 5.2). The dog can also be encouraged to ignore shed equipment and stay focused on the decoy, and you should not be content until he will out properly off a decoy who has shed a jacket or sleeve and stay focused on the decoy, not the equipment (see Figures 5.3, 5.4, 5.5, 5.6, and 5.7).

Trainers who wish to avoid the use of toys and games can do so easily with this method, and those who wish to use them can

Figure 5.1 Muzzled dog engaging the decoy.

Figure 5.2 Unable to hang on, the dog outs properly.

add them every time the dog stops being aggressive. This adds great flexibility to the technique and allows trainers to use their creativity to add their own personal touch to it without lessening its effectiveness.

Figure 5.3 Decoy shedding jacket on a muzzled dog.

Figure 5.4 The dog ignores the shed jacket, outs properly, and stays focused on the decoy.

Figure 5.5 Still ignoring the jacket, the dog re-engages the decoy.

Figure 5.6 Again the dog outs properly without focusing on the equipment.

Figure 5.7 Another look at the focus of the dog.

Rewarding without the Bite

One of the myths associated with muzzle work is that the dog must have the muzzle removed and be allowed to bite frequently or the dog will suffer. While there is nothing wrong with giving the dog a bite at the end of a muzzle routine, the dog will not suffer without it if the decoy involved understands how to properly reward dogs that are working in muzzle. The bite is not the major reward for aggressive behavior; it is the tool the dog uses to obtain the major reward. For instance, if the dog is working in social aggression, the major reward is to see submissive behavior in the other animal. If the dog must bite to get that, he will, but using other tools is also acceptable. If your muzzle decoys are skillful in showing complete submission, this behavior will reward the dog even more than a bite, and the dog will not suffer. For further discussion on this, refer to *K9 Decoys and Aggression: A Manual for Training Police Dogs.*

As with other methods, some dogs learn a behavior well and then just stop doing it correctly. At this point a reasonable punishment should be applied, but this should not be needed often and the severity should not be great. If severe punishments are needed frequently, you are doing something wrong. Go back and check what you are doing.

6

Toys and Games

Many trainers have found playing with the dog's favorite toy to be beneficial as a reward and motivator in obedience, agility, article search, building search, area search, tracking, trailing, and detection work, and in the early 1980s, I started using them for teaching aggression control, as well. Properly selected dogs that are mentally suitable for the work have shown time and time again that they can learn control using toys and still ignore them to fight a human adversary when given the chance.

Properly selected dogs that are mentally suitable for the work have shown time and time again that they can learn control using toys and still ignore them to fight a human adversary when given the chance.

Preparation

Preparation for this style of training includes proper obedience work as described in Chapter 2, so go back and make sure you have completed everything mentioned there. Be certain the dog is solid on the behaviors you want after she releases or terminates the attack. Many dogs are tempted to re-bite after they release because they don't know what to do next and are left hanging. It is a big advantage for them to have a solid idea of what comes next before they get into release training. This uses the technique of "back chaining," where behaviors are linked together but taught in reverse order so the dog always knows how to succeed in what comes next (see page 24 for a discussion of this technique). The dog should also be solid at releasing toys (especially tug toys) from her mouth, even when she is excited.

It is important for the dog to understand that when she releases, she will get a reward that she really likes and that she is not giving up something for nothing. She either gets the same toy back relatively soon, or she gets a different toy or a different game, but she should always get something of high value, not just a little pat on the head. When she can release her toy willingly and trust her handler to provide something else that is just as much fun as the original toy, you can finally add biting the human.

Most dogs will have no difficulty with this if you are using a command they already know and they anticipate a good reward for when they comply. Many dogs respond well to an exciting game of tug of war. Others have obsessions for other toys or games, and this is the time to use them. If from day one the dog has been expected to behave properly around decoys and the rules of obedience have never changed, no matter the location or circumstance, your efforts will really pay off now. Be certain that your decoy does not overly excite the dog, and make sure the dog has enough time to think clearly before you ask for the release. If you have not taught a release command for the toy, you can use some other obedience command such as "Down," so that the dog understands what is expected of her.

Proofing off the toys can be accomplished later by having the decoy toss toys and immediately attempt to escape or attack the dog and handler. Or other people can throw toys into the situation just before the decoy attacks. The dog will soon learn to keep her attention on the decoy. This will not cause much difficulty if the dog was properly proofed off toys in obedience. The dog will soon learn to ignore all toys except those offered by her handler.

Advantages to Toys and Games

There are several advantages to the toys and games approach. It is highly efficient, and more than that, it maintains or improves the relationship between the handler and the dog. The handler is not expecting the dog to give up all her fun just to show control; there is always something good in it for the dog. There is no reason for the dog to cheat or avoid the handler's control.

There is also great flexibility with this technique. It can be done with external sleeves, hidden sleeves, bite suits, or in muzzle (as long as the dog enjoys games and toys in the muzzle). It can be done by using a dropped sleeve as the toy or without dropping sleeves at all. It can be done by teaching the dog to release her toy first, as described above, or without such preparation. It has worked well both ways, depending upon the dog involved.

Proofing Against Training Patterns

Another valuable training concept is "proofing against" the patterns you may have used to teach a behavior. You want to break up patterns in the environment so that they will not control the dog. For instance, Chapter 2 mentions the need to have the fully suited decoy around during obedience so that his presence does not necessarily set a pattern that produces aggressive behavior. We want the *behavior* of the decoy to create aggression, not simply his *presence* or his clothes and equipment. Failure to separate the decoy from the actions that justify aggression produces dogs that become aggressive as soon as decoys walk onto the field. This will cause problems later when it is time to teach aggression control.

To be tactically sound, a dog must respond to the actions of the decoy and the commands of her handler; nothing else should control her. To achieve this, you need to engage in what trainers call "conflict training," where you do things in different ways to break up any patterns you may have set in the dog's mind that may limit her ability to respond properly to unpredictable circumstances. When they are successful, the commands of the handler and the actions of the decoy have what behaviorists refer to as "stimulus control," where nothing else controls the dog's behavior. Examples of things to proof against include equipment, the presence or absence of certain people, the presence of other dogs, different locations, positioning and behavior of the handler, terrain differences, different types of buildings, different footing, different noises, and so on. The list is extensive, and each of us should make our own so that we don't forget the items that are important in our own context.

Balance Rewards and Corrections

As when using other techniques, a small number of dogs learn complex behaviors through chaining well and then just stop doing it. This tendency is minimized if the proper balance of rewards and corrections is maintained throughout each module, or link in the chain. It may be necessary to administer a reasonable punishment occasionally, but the dog should be highly rewarded when she finally complies. This is no different than in other types of training where you need an occasional correction. Again, aggression is just another form of behavior. The rules of behavior do not go out the window simply because we are dealing with aggression. What does go out the window is the need for severe corrections on a frequent basis. The punishments applied should be reasonable and not needed very often, if at all.

Aggression is just another form of behavior. The rules of behavior do not go out the window simply because we are dealing with aggression. What does go out the window is the need for severe corrections on a frequent basis.

Variation: Not Dropping the Sleeve

To avoid dropping sleeves, trainers can try the adaptation used by John Brannon. In this variation of the back-chaining technique, the handler begins with obedience using toys as the reward. You then move to a variable reward schedule as soon as possible (this is where the handler does not reward the dog every time she does something correctly, but randomly, so that she doesn't need the toy every time and can't predict when it will be given again). When the dog is performing consistently, you begin to proof the dog off the toys, starting with the False Start. When the dog is in a heel position, the handler throws the toy but does not release the dog to chase it. When the dog holds position, the handler rewards her with a second toy.

When the dog is performing well on this, she can progress to the Recall, where the handler throws the toy, releases the dog to chase it, but then recalls her. She must stop chasing the toy and return to the handler. The long line may be used here, but gently. The handler should run alongside the dog, using the line only to smoothly slow the dog down. At this point you also teach the Here from a Distance. The dog should now be doing consistent off-leash obedience with toys thrown all over the ground.

This creates a clear concept in the dog's mind that everything comes from or is withheld by her handler and that this is normal. The dog is not allowed to start or terminate a behavior without the handler's approval. This will be a great advantage later when the dog will encounter severe distractions.

ADD IN TUG PLAY AND TRADE

When the obedience rate is at least 80 percent efficient, the handler adds in tug play. First, the handler lets the dog play with and win the tug toy. Next, the handler produces a second tug toy and trades the dog for the original tug (Figures 6.1, 6.2, and 6.3). This begins what is known as the "trade game." Making a trade is not usually a problem, since the original tug is not moving

Figure 6.1 The handler playing tug of war with one hand while producing a second tug toy with the other.

Figure 6.2 The handler presenting the second tug.

Figure 6.3 The handler giving the dog the second tug in trade for the first one.

Figure 6.4 The dog focusing only on the handler and what he offers.

(it is "dead") and the handler is wiggling and moving the second tug (it is "alive"). The dog can then be proofed off all toys and distractions so that she focuses on what the handler offers and nothing else (Figure 6.4).

The next step is to have the dog release the tug during a game of tug of war and let her re-bite the same tug as her reward. When the dog is doing this well with her handler, have her play the game with someone other than her handler. As the dog progresses, vary the handler's distance and location so that the dog doesn't care where he/she is or how far away he/she may be.

At this point the dog is comfortable working for toys, has never been allowed to refuse the handler in anything, is proofed off toys so that she will not be looking for them at inappropriate times, and is comfortable trading a stationary or moving tug toy for either a second tug or a re-bite of the same one. The foundations have now been laid to play the trade game with a decoy (Figures 6.5 and 6.6). Note that this game can be done with sleeve drops or without ever dropping a sleeve, as the trainer desires. It could be done in a bite suit or not; it is a flexible technique. Work slowly in small increments and do not be content until you have a dog that will ignore toys, sleeves, suits, and

Figure 6.5 The dog should attack with full intensity and bite well.

Figure 6.6 The dog trading the decoy for her tug and a game with the handler.

anything else you can think of (Figures 6.7, 6.8, 6.9, and 6.10) in order to pursue a person. Eventually, the dog will be able to start a pursuit with a tug toy in her mouth, pursue the decoy at full speed past multiple tugs on the ground, and bite the decoy with

Figure 6.7 The dog ignoring toys, tugs, and suits to focus on a high back bite.

Figure 6.8 The dog preparing to engage the decoy. Note toys, sleeves, and bite suits on the ground, as well as tugs tied to and carried by the decoy.

Figure 6.9 The dog ignoring the proofing materials as the decoy presents himself for an inside arm bite.

Figure 6.10 The dog ignoring the tugs tied to and carried by the decoy and biting the man hard on the inside of the arm.

full intensity even though the decoy has been tossing more tugs at the dog as she approaches.

No method is magic and none will work perfectly on all dogs. The above method has proven itself with good dogs under the guidance of a good trainer and is offered as a starting point if you have never used this type of training. If your dog needs something slightly different, hang on to the basic principles and adjust the details of what you are doing to suit the animal you have.

Controversy over Sleeve Dropping

The method of slipping or dropping sleeves is a controversial one since when it is done improperly, it can produce "sleeve happy" dogs that are strongly focused on the sleeve or other protective equipment. Such dogs and will often ignore the human adversary in order to "win" the equipment, putting their handlers at risk in real-life situations. It will probably remain controversial for some time. For descriptions of how to use sleeve drops in ways that focus the dog back on the human adversary, refer to *K9 Decoys and Aggression: A*

Manual for Training Police Dogs. The process described above can be used without ever dropping a sleeve and is well-suited to trainers who are not in favor of sleeve dropping. Those trainers who like to drop sleeves may prefer the following approach.

> The topic of slipping or dropping sleeves is a controversial one and will probably remain so for some time. The method described above can be used without ever dropping a sleeve and is well-suited to trainers who are not in favor of sleeve dropping.

Variation: Dropping the Sleeve

Those trainers who like to drop sleeves may prefer the variation used by trainer Bill Nott. Instead of trading a tug for another tug, first, the decoy drops the sleeve, and after the dog carries it around for a while, she trades the sleeve for a tug toy. The process begins with obedience using some other toy than a tug, saving the tug for bite work. When bite work begins, each session starts with tolerance drills, during which the dog is expected to stay calm while the decoy behaves in a loud, boisterous manner. If obedience has been done properly, as described in Chapter 2, the dog should be well-prepared for this. When the dog remains calm even when tempted, and the handler can issue all types of announcements and challenges, the dog is rewarded with a tug toy.

> When bite work begins, each session starts with tolerance drills, during which the dog is expected to stay calm while the decoy behaves in a loud, boisterous manner.

BITE DRILL

When the dog is down and quiet, the bite drill can begin. As soon as she has a good, full-mouth bite, the decoy slips the sleeve off and the dog is allowed to carry it around for a while. Then the handler produces a tug, made more interesting than the motionless sleeve when the handler wiggles and moves it around. The dog will drop the sleeve and take the tug (see Figures 6.11, 6.12, 6.13, 6.14, and 6.15). Perform this type of "transfer" (from the sleeve to the tug) after the bite three times, and on the third time every person present should gather, allowing the dog carry her prize (the tug) through the crowd while everyone makes a big

Figure 6.11 The dog should pursue the decoy with full intensity.

Figure 6.12 The dog should commit fully to a good bite.

Figure 6.13 The decoy slipping the sleeve after the handler has the short lead.

Figure 6.14 The dog transfers to the tug toy after carrying the sleeve for a while.

Figure 6.15 Transfer complete.

fuss over the dog and lets her show off. The handler never takes the sleeve or the tug from the dog. The dog never loses anything and no avoidance behavior develops. Before the dog gets into the car, she must release the tug for a different toy (not a tug), signifying that the tug game is over. Remember not to force the issue; be patient.

The next step is to move the handler back and allow the dog to work in front of the handler. After each bite and transfer, the handler returns the sleeve to the decoy and puts it back on him. The decoy is never allowed to take the sleeve back or to try to steal the sleeve from the dog. Competition between the dog and the decoy is not helpful at this point in training since you are trying to get the dog to voluntarily give up the sleeve. If this process is done properly, the dog will soon begin looking for the tug while she is still carrying the sleeve, anticipating and enjoying the transfer. It is then time to move to the next phase.

> **After each bite and transfer, the handler returns the sleeve to the decoy and puts it back on him. The decoy is never allowed to take the sleeve back or to try to steal the sleeve from the dog. Competition between the dog and the decoy is not helpful at this point in training since you are trying to get the dog to voluntarily give up the sleeve.**

The next phase continues the tolerance drills with increased intensity until the decoy can stand directly in front of the dog screaming and moving and the dog will not bite until given a command. If she then bites well and transfers from the sleeve to a tug without difficulty, it is time to move on again.

POSITIONING

Positioning is the next item to work on. Place a decoy in the center of an area and have him pretend to be standing on the center of a round clock face. The dog is placed in a Down on one of the hour number positions and the handler moves to another hour position. The handler then calls the dog to the new position or downs her anywhere along the way. By mixing up the sequences in this, the handler gains great control in positioning the dog during drills and real encounters. If obedience has been properly taught, as described in Chapter 2, the dog will be well-prepared for this step.

RECALL

The recall comes next. This begins with a baby recall, where the decoy holding a tug jogs a few steps away, stops, and turns to face the dog. The dog downs, with help from the handler if necessary, and the decoy throws the tug over the dog's head (so she must turn away from the decoy to see where it has landed). Then the dog retrieves the tug, and the handler plays with the dog. The distance is increased (using long lines) to at least 50 feet (15 m), and tolerance drills are continued throughout the phases. Now the decoy is given a sleeve, and when the dog downs on the recall, the decoy comes to the dog for a bite, which still results in a sleeve drop and transfer to a tug.

FINAL STEP

Lastly, the dog needs to transfer from a sleeve that just happens to be on a man's arm, but she is now well-prepared to do so. Dogs are famous for anticipating the next task in a sequence and jumping to the next step even before it is time to do so. This tendency works in our favor for once. For some time now the dog has been looking for the tug while carrying the sleeve and when the sleeve stays on the decoy's arm, she is quite willing to cheat and jump to the next step, transferring off the man to the tug (see Figures 6.16, 6.17, 6.18, 6.19, and 6.20). Naturally, this requires a competent decoy who knows enough not to stimulate the dog when it is time to transfer (or just before). (That said, a good decoy is a requirement for all training styles.) Variety is important once the dog understands the drill. Give rewards on

Figure 6.16 Full intensity pursuit. Good dogs do not look for toys.

Figure 6.17 Good dogs still use hard, full-mouth bites with these techniques.

Figure 6.18 The dog anticipating the transfer, except this time the sleeve is on the man.

Figure 6.19 The dog completes the transfer to the tug.

Figure 6.20 The result: after a pursuit and bite, the handler calls the dog out from a distance while he stays under cover.

a random or intermittent schedule so the handler does not have to have the reward with him all the time and doesn't need to use the primary reward in a real situation. Training is not complete until the dog is proofed off the tug toys.

Dogs are famous for anticipating the next task in a sequence and jumping to the next step even before it is time to do so. This tendency works in our favor for once.

Potential Problems

The above techniques offer great advantages over the older, more compulsive techniques, but there are still some ways to mess them up. For example, if the wrong toy or game is used, it will not create enough motivation in the dog to produce the behavior you want. It is important to take time in the beginning of training to identify the exact toy or game the dog values the most. Then make sure this is what the dog is being offered for the trade or transfer.

Another mistake trainers make is improperly or incompletely proofing the dog off the toys. Enough dogs have been trained with these techniques now to demonstrate that the use of toys and games do not cause problems in good dogs that have been properly trained. If your finished dogs are looking for toys, examine your canine-selection procedures and your proofing abilities.

Enough dogs have been trained with these techniques now to demonstrate that the use of toys and games do not cause problems in good dogs that have been properly trained. If your finished dogs are looking for toys, examine your canine-selection procedures and your proofing abilities.

DOGS WITH SENSORY OVERLOAD

A few dogs out there have trouble with overexcitability, what is sometimes called *sensory overload*. When they get above a certain level of excitement, they cannot think or act in a controlled manner. Sometimes this is a result of a traumatic event, and sometimes it is just the natural condition for the dog, which means in some animals it is a temporary condition and with others it is a lifelong problem. Regardless of its duration or cause, these animals must be treated in a dull, boring manner to keep their excitement at levels where they can perform well (see Chapter 1 on the Yerkes-Dodson Law). The pain of a punishment creates excitement in such dogs and needs to be avoided for training to progress. Most of the techniques described in this book will provide aggression control without using pain as the primary tool. Of course, a good game with the right toy is also exciting and can cause a loss of control. It doesn't matter to these dogs what the source of excitement is, pain or pleasure—they can't handle either. So with these dogs we must avoid games and toys as well as pain until they gain the ability to handle excitement. If you are dealing with a dog that has a genetic disposition for sensory overload, know that she will never gain this ability.

You are more likely to see this type of dog now than you were years ago, since we are experiencing an industry-wide problem with recognizing the difference between high levels of motivation and wildness. A highly motivated dog has high levels of energy in her approach to work, but the energy is focused and the dog can think clearly at all times. In a desire to obtain an energetic dog, some trainers are accepting dogs that have high energy levels but no focus and a tendency to lose the ability to reason when they begin to work. This is simply wildness and has no place in police work. Police dogs need to be able to think to solve problems in their everyday work. This is one of the major differences between police and other dogs, and we must not allow it to be forgotten or passed over. If you are unfortunate enough to have to train such a dog, keep everything dull and boring to keep the dog at a reasonable level of excitement, and you will have much greater success.

In a desire to obtain an energetic dog, some trainers are accepting dogs that have high energy levels but no focus and a tendency to lose the ability to reason when they begin to work. This is simply wildness and has no place in police work. Police dogs need to be able to think to solve problems in their everyday work.

Benefits of Positive Training

Some dogs get dirty and start cheating after they get their first bite in the real world. This is a minor problem with dogs trained in the above manner since they already know what the correct behavior is. A small number of standard corrections straighten them out and are often unnecessary thereafter. Abusive levels of pain are not required. Remember that behaviors taught with positive-reinforcement techniques last longer and are generally more reliable than those taught with punishment. Behaviorists have long known that punishment is a temporary tool, and unless it is completely traumatic, its effects do not last long. Therefore, many dogs need to be "cleaned up" on a regular basis since they were trained with punishment as the major training tool. Using positive reinforcement really pays off now since the dogs are more willing to return to the behaviors we want and its effects last much longer.

CASE EXAMPLE: REX

The scene was a national training workshop in North Carolina in the month of June. The weather was hot and humid as you might imagine. In fact, everything was as you would imagine except that one of the instructors in aggression control was teaching the use of toys and games as a reward for the release after the bite. Since this was a rare occurrence at the time, it attracted a certain amount of attention, even from handlers who were merely observing and had not brought their dogs.

One of these handlers worked for a rural sheriff's office and had been watching other people's dogs working for some time without saying a word. Finally, he approached the instructor and asked if he would still be around in another hour. Apparently, he wanted to drive home and return with his dog but did not want to return and find the instructor gone. The instructor assured him he would remain on the field until the handler returned, and work resumed on other dogs.

Sure enough, an hour later the handler returned and introduced the instructor to Rex (not his real name). Rex was a young, medium-sized male German shepherd dog. He was sable in color, and his story was a familiar one. He performed well in everything else but had never outed properly, even in basic school. No amount of compulsion seemed to be enough to change his mind, and the handler eventually resigned himself to the fact that he would have to work this dog carefully and hope that he would never have to call him off anyone. The handler developed the habit of not bringing Rex to seminars, but when he saw the positive results the instructor was getting with everyone else's dogs, he decided to give this new approach a try.

The instructor asked the handler to get Rex's favorite toy, so the handler went back to his vehicle, took out a common tennis ball, and returned. Rex was given a bite and the handler was positioned so that Rex could see both the decoy and the handler. The decoy kept the excitement to a minimum, and when the handler showed the tennis ball and gave the out command, Rex popped right off the sleeve the very first time and returned to the handler, who immediately gave him his favorite game.

As with many dogs, Rex had never wanted to be a problem; he simply had not been set up properly to succeed and had never been offered a decent substitute for the decoy. When he was given a chance, he turned out to be no problem at all. These techniques do not always work as quickly as they did in Rex's case, but they often do, and Rex's story is not too unusual.

CASE EXAMPLE: RUGER

Ruger (not his real name) was a large, black, male German shepherd dog who had always been a problem in aggression control. He had an excellent trainer and good decoys but had always required heavy doses of electricity to work, and even then, things were difficult. When he knew electricity was coming, he would stiffen his neck, scream, and bite harder instead of releasing. Only the most massive amounts of electricity would convince Ruger to be compliant. He was never really reliable, and the trainer was never really happy with the situation.

After much discussion, the trainer decided to give toys and games a try since compulsion was not yielding the results he wanted. It was decided to use a variation of the sleeve-transfer method with four different sleeves. The sleeves were placed in separate locations. The decoy put on the first sleeve and gave the dog a bite. The decoy slipped the sleeve and Ruger was allowed to carry the sleeve around.

During this time, the decoy slowly moved to the second location and put on the second sleeve. The handler then brought Ruger over and positioned him in front of the decoy and waited for the dog to drop the first sleeve, which was still in his mouth. As soon as Ruger dropped the first sleeve, he was immediately given a bite on the second sleeve and allowed to carry it around when it, too, was slipped. During this time, the decoy moved to the third sleeve and put it on. The handler positioned Ruger in front of the decoy again, and when the dog dropped the second sleeve, he was immediately given a bite with the third sleeve, which was slipped so he could carry it around as well.

After Ruger was transferred to the fourth sleeve in a similar manner and was allowed to carry it around, he was transferred off the sleeve to a tug in the normal manner and the session was over. Ruger began to anticipate and enjoy the transfers, and after three sessions with the four sleeves was outing normally off the decoy with no sleeve slipping and no electricity.

7

Decoys and Equipment

The most important tool a trainer has is a good decoy. From the first day of obedience training, the decoy should be present, but he must behave neutrally. For the decoy to become a neutral stimulus, he should be fully dressed as a decoy but act normally, so that the dog has no reason to focus on him. You are trying to teach the dog that it is the *behavior* of the decoy that determines whether or not he should be bitten, not the clothes or equipment he is wearing. The lesson will not be complete until aggression training begins, but you set up a good foundation for training if you begin by showing the dog a nonaggressive decoy and rewarding the dog for behaving normally around him.

Decoys make or break the dog, particularly in sensitive parts of training. They must be skilled communicators and have good coordination and timing. They must also understand the Yerkes-Dodson Law (see Chapter 1) and how their actions move the dog along the inverted U. Loading the dog by using exciting movements or signals at the wrong time will destroy everything the trainer is trying to accomplish. For this reason, many trainers learn how to decoy and play the role themselves to minimize mistakes and avoid arguments with decoys, which is one of the biggest problems a trainer can have.

For some reason, many decoys reach a stage of development where they feel they know more than the trainer. To become useful, a decoy must work through this phase of development, but some never make it. They spend the rest of their careers arguing with trainers about what should be done with their dogs. Their physical skills are worthless at this point since trainers cannot trust them to do what they're told. If you are working with a decoy who will not do exactly what you ask when he disagrees with you, it would be better for you to get a new decoy, particularly if his actions are placing the dog in the wrong part of the inverted U. Nothing good comes from a decoy exciting the dog at the wrong time.

If you are working with a decoy who will not do exactly as you ask when he disagrees with you, it would be better for you to get a new decoy, particularly if his actions are placing the dog in the wrong part of the inverted U.

Signals

Decoys should always use signals appropriate to what the trainer is trying to accomplish. This is particularly true when you are working on the release. If a decoy uses challenging signals immediately before or during the time that a handler is giving the release command, he is working against the trainer at a time when he should be helping. Many dogs dominate the decoy during the biting process and if the subordinate animal (the decoy) challenges them, it will motivate the dogs to continue biting to maintain their dominance. Challenging signals are appropriate in many phases of training, but decoys should switch to submissive signals when the trainer is teaching the release.

Challenging signals are appropriate in many phases of training, but decoys should switch to submissive signals when the trainer is teaching the release.

DISTANCE-INCREASING SIGNALS

Communication and signaling between the decoy and the dog are discussed in *K9 Decoys and Aggression: A Manual for Training Police Dogs*. Only upper-ranking animals are allowed to use what are known as "distance-increasing" signals. In the world of dogs these "go-away" signals are considered challenges, and lower-ranking animals are not allowed to use them. If they do, it is the upper-ranking dog's job to maintain order in the pack by punishing the offender. Since dogs punish the offenders by biting them, it is not good for the decoy to use these signals when the trainer is trying to encourage the dog to stop biting. To be helpful when the trainer is teaching the release, decoys should avoid distance-increasing signals such as quick, exciting movements; facing the dog squarely; direct eye contact; and towering over the dog. They should instead use submissive signals: standing still for inspection; rotating their bodies sideways as much as possible; breaking eye contact; and lowering their bodies slightly.

Handler Mistakes

Decoys should always be flexible and willing to adapt their actions to surprise situations. Handlers are just as prone to making mistakes as anyone else, especially under pressure. Sometimes handlers give the wrong commands or the right commands at the wrong times. Even when these commands are completely contrary to the training plan, no matter how well said plan was discussed, they are still commands and cannot be ignored without consequence. It is the decoy's job to support the handler's commands with the appropriate actions and let the trainer deal with the consequences. Even when the handler is getting it wrong, the actions of the decoy and the handler should always be synchronized, and hopefully the handler will get better at following the trainer's directions. Again, handlers are the trainer's responsibility, not the decoy's. The decoy's job is to synchronize with the handler, unless the trainer gives him direct orders to the contrary.

Positioning

How the decoy positions the dog is important. As we know from obedience, dogs think differently when their handlers are either out of range or somehow physically blocked from reaching them. We seem to get better behavior when a dog realizes that his handler has direct access to him. This is particularly true if the dog has a competitive relationship with his handler. A dog that likes to cheat or compete with his handler tends to do so more when he is out of the handler's reach than when he knows his handler can touch him.

During bite work, this can lead to the dog spinning the decoy around so that the dog is positioned on the far side of the decoy when he doesn't want his handler to interfere, such as when the dog knows the release command is coming and he doesn't want to let go just yet. Any time the dog wants to be independent of the handler during bite work, he will try to spin the decoy around to get away from the handler. So to contribute to success, the decoy must keep the dog from spinning him and keep the dog positioned so that the dog is directly between the decoy and the handler. This gives the handler direct physical access to the dog and encourages the dog to think more cooperatively.

> To contribute to training success, the decoy must keep the dog from spinning him and keep the dog positioned so that the dog is directly between the decoy and the handler.

The decoy should always inform the trainer that the dog is trying to get away from the handler since this indicates an improper relationship between the two and that there is some underlying issue that needs to be addressed. Problems range anywhere between simple competition to the dog feeling the handler's presence is a threat and he is trying to get away from him to avoid the bad treatment the dog has received in the past. Whatever the cause, something needs to be improved, but this is a job for the trainer not the decoy. The decoy's job is merely to inform the trainer of the dog's desire to spin him.

Relationship between Dog and Decoy

The general relationship between the dog and the decoy can sometimes cause trouble. When sleeve dropping is used, some trainers encourage the decoy to try to steal the dropped sleeve back from the dog after it has been dropped. This creates a more possessive frame of mind in the dog and often produces a dog that will fight harder for the sleeve and score higher in competition. While this is an advantage for some sport dogs, it creates a strongly competitive relationship between the dog and the decoy that can cause problems when the dog is expected to release.

Generally, it is not an advantage to have a dog obsessively fighting for possession of the sleeve when you are trying to teach the Out. Instead you want the dog to give up the sleeve and stop competing with the decoy. If you have set up too much competition and desire for the sleeve in the dog, it will really hurt you when it comes time to teach the Out. For this reason, many trainers are moving away from the old techniques, such as leaving the sleeve on the ground in front of the dog and having the decoy try to steal it back. They now look ahead and plan for the day when they must teach the release; and when they do this, things go much better.

Equipment

Sometimes switching equipment provides you and your dogs with an advantage. Some dogs have a habit of getting their teeth caught in the sleeve or bite suit and cannot release even when they choose to. This often happens when the material is worn out and frayed. Occasionally all you have to do is use better equipment to help the dog learn what you are trying to teach. Whenever you get the impression that the dog is trying to release but is having difficulty, it is worth your while to switch the type of equipment you are using before you give up. In other cases, dogs may be more willing to release when they are working on hard hidden sleeves than when you are using soft jute material. Also, check your dog to make sure he will release from all the different types of equipment. If you only use certain types of equipment when teaching the release, the dog may not realize that you want him to release from other types. Dogs that generalize well will have no problems, but those that discriminate well can become confused when you set a pattern regarding equipment.

Occasionally all you have to do is use better equipment to help the dog learn what you are trying to teach. Whenever you get the impression that the dog is trying to release but is having difficulty, it is worth your while to switch the type of equipment you are using before you give up.

Old Memories

Old memories can also cause complications. If the dog's previous trainer expected wild, undisciplined behavior when a certain piece of equipment was used, the dog may not understand that you expect something different in the presence of that same equipment. This often occurs with the bite suit. Since people feel a little safer when using one, they frequently encourage the dog to be a little wilder when using one. Sometimes this complicates the teaching of the release since the mere presence of a bite suit excites the dog more than any other type of equipment. The muzzle can have this same effect if it is only used during aggression work.

Decoys must be physically skilled, good at positioning, good communicators, and willing to follow instructions even when they disagree with the trainer. If they are not, your dog will have difficulty learning aggression control. If you do not have a good decoy, make finding one a top priority. Good decoys are worth their weight in gold.

CASE EXAMPLE: SHEP

Shep (not his real name) was a German shepherd dog who began his life in Europe as a working dog candidate, and relatively little is known or remembered about him before he was selected by an importer and flown to the United States. Like hundreds of dogs before him, Shep was examined by several people, most of whom recognized that he had all the necessary qualities to become a good police dog. Eventually, he found himself enrolled in a basic patrol dog school of the K9 unit of a large city on the east coast. His handler was as talented as most new handlers, and while no K9 team is ever perfect, Shep and his handler posed no great problems as they progressed through school. They soon graduated and were put to work on the streets of the city.

Everything was going fine until at some point they were forced to physically engage a very large male suspect who was clearly committed to resisting arrest. The suspect was inside a room, and as soon as Shep made contact, the man turned his attention to the dog and the fight was on. More than once during the prolonged fight, Shep was thrown through the air to smash against the nearest wall and slide down to the floor. More than once Shep picked himself up and hurled himself back into the fight. Many dogs would have quit under this kind of stress, but Shep's genetics were good, he was well-raised and -trained, and he was not about to give up easily. Eventually, the suspect was subdued and taken into custody. Shep had performed magnificently and was a complete credit to his breeder, his importer, his trainer, and his handler, but he was never the same again.

The stress and trauma of the event had changed the way Shep thought about and related to people and the world in general. He became unpredictable (except for the fact that he would not release a decoy) and was so dangerous to be around that the city was forced to consider taking him off the street. This would have been more than the loss of a good dog: it would have been the loss of a great deal of time and money as well. I knew that something was outside the normal when I was asked to evaluate Shep because the trainer was one of the best in the business and did not need help training a dog. So it was time to focus on the decoys to see how they fit into the equation.

It was soon evident that changing the behavior of the decoys might help. They were working Shep in the same manner they had before the fight, whereas his needs had changed. What used to be a healthy amount of stimulation was now too much for him and was pushing him over the top of the inverted U into the right side where performance deteriorates (see Chapter 1 on the Yerkes-Dodson Law).

Shep's enemy was excitement, and the only people who could help him were his decoys. Once the trainer realized this, he changed the decoys' routines to incorporate slower movements, less challenging signals, and no fighting during the bite itself, making bite work quite boring. However, this held Shep's excitement down to a level where the dog could think, and he began to learn that he was still capable of handling difficult situations. As Shep's confidence in his own abilities began to rise back to where it had been before the fight, his behavior became more confident and predictable, with the added benefit that he began to release decoys again. The boring behavior of the decoys shifted the dog to the left on the inverted U, and his performance rose back to previous levels.

As time passed, the decoys found they could shift their behavior back to normal, and, as long as they didn't do anything too wild, Shep continued to out off the bad guy. While it is not always possible to reclaim dogs after bad experiences, the decoys are often a critical element in the process. In this case, they helped a good dog overcome the effects of a traumatic experience and saved their city a lot of money at the same time.

8

Problem Solving

Many complications arise when teaching the dog to release after the bite, but some are seen more frequently than others. Problems that cause complications include the following:

- starting with a dog that is too wild for this kind of work in the first place;
- not preparing the dog properly during obedience;
- having a decoy who places the dog in the wrong part of the inverted U (see Chapter 1 on the Yerkes-Dodson Law);
- using equipment that overexcites the dog; and
- a competitive relationship between dog and handler.

While these are all seen frequently, by far the most commonly seen problem is that of using too much pain and punishment in the training process. This book is an attempt to emphasize techniques that avoid this problem by minimizing or eliminating the need for pain and punishment during training. Keep in mind that the rules of operant conditioning do not go out the window simply because we are dealing with aggression. All the rules of behavioral science are still in effect, and if they work on animals like killer whales (which they do), they will certainly work on aggressive dogs.

Although the Self Out, game playing, and the use of toys work best on untrained dogs in initial training, these methods were not originally designed for green dogs. When I first developed these processes in the late 1970s and early 1980s, they were used with dogs that had control problems. Most of these dogs reacted badly to severe punishments, which at that time were routinely used for teaching control. It was only later that trainers realized how effective these pain-free techniques are with green dogs.

Eliminate Triggers and Reinforcers

Dog trainers have had good success over the years when addressing problem behaviors by identifying and eliminating the triggers (the stimuli that cause an animal to exhibit a certain behavior) and the reinforcers. This allows the problem behaviors to extinguish (disappear) and lets the trainers reinforce or reward a behavior that is more to their liking. In aggression control, pain is often the trigger for our problems. In many cases, simply eliminating pain as the major teaching tool significantly improves the situation.

The type of dog we select for aggression work is not the kind of animal that gives up easily. When confronted with a problem, a good candidate dog will keep working to solve it. If the problem is a handler who is being unreasonable, the dog will keep working to solve this problem as well, even when severe punishments are involved. Dogs with high pain tolerances can survive severe punishments and learn to compete with and fight against the handler. This encourages them to cheat during aggression control to beat the handler and get what they want. In many cases the root of this whole problem is the severe punishment and the dog's reaction to the pain.

> **Dogs with a high pain tolerance can survive severe punishments and learn to compete with and fight against the handler. This encourages them to cheat during aggression control to beat the handler and get what they want. In many cases the root of this whole problem is the severe punishment and the dog's reaction to the pain.**

What if we remove pain from the process entirely? The dog would have nothing to react badly to, and every behavior that is a result of the bad reaction would disappear. This is the basis of the Self Out, game playing, and using toys. When we avoid the bad reactions to severe punishment, training becomes more effective. Add to this a good relationship between dog and handler, established during obedience (see Chapter 2), and teaching aggression control becomes much easier. The quality of the dog's life also improves.

Most of the tough, well-bred dogs that are selected for working purposes are quite intelligent for their species. They do not need severe punishments to learn and enjoy their jobs. Give them a competent leader who does not abuse them and they will learn aggression control easily and perform at levels that will astound most people. Start a fight with them and you have a substantial enemy to deal with. Most will fight you to the bitter end. In many cases, they are better fighters than we are, and we lose. We end up with a resentful, contentious dog that cheats at every opportunity. Fortunately, this is not necessary and can be completely avoided by following the advice in this book. By using the techniques described in the previous chapters, you can have a dog that learns quickly, performs reliably, respects her leader, and enjoys life. It's a good deal.

Avoid the Quick Fix

The techniques described in this book often work quite quickly, but some dogs require more repetitions. When dealing with problem behaviors, we should be cautious of quick fixes. What we want is a long-lasting change, not a partial fix that appears quickly but fades away just as fast. This quick fading is often what we get when we use punishment as the major training tool. As stated before, punishment is a temporary tool; its results do not last long unless some form of trauma is involved. Many dogs whose control training was largely comprised of punishment need to be retrained or "cleaned up" frequently. Behaviors created and reinforced positively usually show better reliability and longevity, and we have definitely seen this in aggression control work.

Unfortunately, trainers who want to use the techniques described in this book are often put under time pressure. They are often presented with problem dogs and are given only a few days to turn the dogs around, so at seminars they try to use a quick fix. What everyone forgets is that it took many repetitions to create the problems and it may take more than just a few repetitions of good techniques to counteract the problems in any meaningful way. A quick fix is easier to accomplish in a short time frame, and this is what most trainers choose to do. We need to encourage trainers to demonstrate good, long-lasting techniques, and let someone else finish the work when they go home. Don't pressure them to give the dog a quick fix that will get her through certification but will fade quickly when she returns home. One of the most important lessons for new trainers is to make time to do things correctly rather than messing things up by trying to take shortcuts.

One of the most important lessons for new trainers is to make time to do things correctly rather than messing things up by trying to take shortcuts.

Avoid Pain-Induced Aggression

As mentioned above, pain-induced aggression plays a major part in many of the problems we face in aggression control. This is a type of aggression whose biological purpose is to increase the survivability of the dog by making pain go away. Pain is a biological warning system that gets the dog's attention and signals that something is wrong and needs to be taken care of immediately. Consequently, making pain disappear often improves the dog's condition and increases her chances of survival.

When dogs with a genetic predisposition for this type of aggression feel pain, they attack what they perceive to be the source. If they think that this aggression helps their cause or actually makes the pain go away, they will repeat the behavior with greater intensity the next time they experience pain. This is the basis of the old, outdated agitation techniques of flanking, pinching, whipping the front legs with sticks, and feeding dogs gunpowder. These techniques created aggression but also created side effects that caused many safety problems for the people who had to live with or service the dogs. Fortunately, we now have better ways to stimulate aggression humanely and do not need to use these old techniques any longer.

Pain-induced aggression has a genetic predisposition and is quite prevalent in dogs. It is one reason that all working dogs should be trained to be comfortable in a nonrestrictive, agitation-type muzzle. Then when they are injured you can muzzle them as a first step without increasing their stress levels. You are then safe to handle and help them without getting bitten in the process. In the first place, however, it hardly makes sense to use a tool that will increase aggression at a time when we are trying to teach the dog to lower her aggression levels. It makes more sense to avoid tools that increase aggression when we are trying to teach control.

Avoid Redirected Aggression

The other form of aggression that complicates control work is what is known as redirected aggression. This is aggression that has been diverted from its preferred target to a secondary target (hence "redirected"). When the dog is biting the decoy, she is doing what she has been trained to do, what she considers to be proper. When the handler starts using pain during this process (in an attempt to get the dog to stop biting), the dog is annoyed, since she is only doing what she has been trained to do.

Many dogs would like to bite the handler at this point, but it is against dog-world rules to bite an upper-ranking animal. The aggression must go somewhere, so the dog looks around for some other target. There is only one lower-ranking animal close at hand to release this aggression on—the decoy. So the dog bites harder. By using pain the trainer and handler have guaranteed that the dog will not lower her aggression level but in fact will bite harder the more pain they inflict on her. Unless you achieve an escape reaction, the dog will simply bite harder and harder, and it is your own fault.

So whether we are dealing with pain-induced aggression or redirected aggression, the use of pain simply raises the aggression levels and works against us. Many of the dogs displaying these behaviors are not trying to be difficult; they are simply being forced into bad behavior by poorly educated humans. Different dogs have different genetic predispositions toward these problems, so we will not always see them in the dogs we train, but many problem dogs are wrestling with these issues. By using the techniques explained in this book, you can give these animals the maximum chance of improving. You will improve the quality of their lives at the same time. If you feel responsible for your dogs, become skillful with less painful training techniques.

Many of these dogs are not trying to be difficult; they are simply being forced into bad behavior by poorly educated humans.

Change Commands

Many dogs improve faster if you change the commands you use for the release and control. The old commands are sounds that may carry old memories and trigger old responses. These old responses are the reason the dog has been brought to you, so you need to leave them behind. Using a different system of training with different commands seems to help many dogs make a smoother transition to new behaviors.

Use Breed-Appropriate Techniques

Sometimes the techniques we are using are not well-suited to the breed of dog we are working with. Many trainers begin their careers working with the German shepherd dog (for good reason) and develop habits and preferences that fit this breed quite well. Some of these habits, however, do not fit other breeds quite as well as they do the German shepherd dog. When you try to force these other breeds into the mold of the German shepherd dog, you can get in trouble.

Sometimes the techniques we are using are not well-suited to the breed of dog we are working with.

Most German shepherds are reasonable animals, so we can bully them into doing things if we are consistent about how we do it. This is not good training for the breed, but we get away with it because of their genetic background. The dog will eventually figure out what we want and has a basic desire to work with her leader.

Other breeds have different genetic backgrounds and do not show this behavior as strongly as the German shepherd dog. Two cases in point are the Rottweiler and the Belgian Malinois. When these breeds first became popular in the United States, we got into trouble with them because we insisted that they behave like the German shepherd. When we used techniques designed to force the German shepherd dog into compliance, these new breeds fought back. Most experienced trainers will agree that if you start fights with Rottweilers or Belgian Malinois, many of them will fight you to the death just out of principle. In an effort to evade responsibility for using poor training techniques, many people tried to blame the dogs by labeling them as "stubborn." In fact, they are not stubborn. If we take the time to motivate them properly with positive techniques, these dogs are not difficult to work with. They simply won't be bullied into things, especially by pain.

If we take the time to motivate dog breeds such as the
Rottweiler or Belgian Malinois properly with positive
techniques, they are not at all difficult to work with.
They simply won't be bullied into things, especially
by pain.

General Questions for Troubleshooting

When you are having trouble teaching a dog to release the decoy,
it might be helpful to go through the following list of items and
discuss them with other experienced trainers:

1. Is the dog in the top of the inverted U? Have you commanded
   the dog at the correct time? Can the dog think clearly? Make
   sure you control the dog's excitement levels properly. Refer to
   Chapter 1 on the Yerkes-Dodson Law. Examine all possible
   sources of excitement.

2. What have you done in obedience to prepare the dog?
   Refer to Chapter 2 and remember that a dog that will not
   release a toy is not ready to release a man.

3. Have you taught the dog, or are you bullying him with
   pain? Have you gone back to the beginning of the teaching
   process? Are you sure the dog understands what you want?

4. Are you fighting old memories? If the dog has previous
   training experience, have you changed the type of location,
   decoys, equipment, training sequences, commands, and
   even the language?

5. Are your techniques well-suited to the breed of dog you are
   working with? Are you trying to force some other breed of
   dog to act like a German shepherd?

6. Is the dog competing with the handler? This competition
   often starts in obedience, so review Chapter 2 and go back
   and reteach if necessary. Look for any tendency of the dog
   to spin the decoy to get away from the handler.

7. Is the handler doing his/her job correctly? Is he/she using the
   correct sequences at the proper time? Is he/she distracting,
   threatening, or creating aggression or confusion in the dog?

8. Is the decoy doing his job correctly? Is he using submissive signals? Is he keeping the dog's excitement levels in the proper range? Is he keeping the dog between the decoy and the handler?

9. Are the handler and the decoy synchronized? Are they both asking for the same thing at the same time?

10. What is rewarding the bad behavior? If a behavior (even a bad behavior) exists, it is being rewarded, so search for the reward and eliminate it.

11. How can you increase the reward for releasing? If a behavior (even a good behavior) does not exist, the dog is not anticipating a sufficient reward, so increase the reward and find a way to get the dog to think it is coming right after the release.

12. Have you set any patterns with locations, sequences, decoys, equipment, and so on that are hurting the process?

13. Have you tried the muzzle? Don't give up until you have. Remember that with any behavior, when the teeth are part of the problem, sometimes the muzzle is part of the solution.

14. As with all problem solving, when everything logical fails, try something illogical (as long as it is humane—this is not to be used as an excuse for abusive treatment—just a change of logic).

Returning to the idea of eliminating the triggers and rein-forcements of problem behaviors, this book should give you more options than the older methods that are still so popular. As you gain more experience with these techniques, you will no doubt add improvements that will increase their effectiveness. This is good as long as we continue to decrease our reliance and dependence upon pain as a teaching tool. We are so much better off now than we were in the old days. We should continue this improvement. This book should be only the beginning.

Index

About the Author

Dr. Stephen A. Mackenzie holds a Ph.D. in the genetics of behavior from Cornell University. He is currently a professor in the Animal Science Department at the State University of New York at Cobleskill, where he teaches Genetics, Canine Training, Care and Training of the Working Dog, and Canine Management. He has been a deputy sheriff for the Schoharie County Sheriff's Office for over 20 years, serving as their K9 handler and trainer for seven years. He is rated a master trainer of utility, cadaver, narcotics, and wildlife detection dogs by the North American Police Work Dog Association (NAPWDA), is an executive board member of North East Wilderness Search and Rescue Inc., is presently serving as the president of the newly established New York State Canine Association, and is the author of *K9 Decoys and Aggression: A Manual for Training Police Dogs* and *Police Officer's Guide to K9 Searches*. "Doc" is a nose work trial judge for the National Association of Canine Scent Work (NACSW), a court-recognized expert in animal behavior at state and federal levels in both criminal and civil cases, and a frequent instructor at police-dog seminars across the United States and Canada.

You can contact Dr. Mackenzie at mackensa@cobleskill.edu.

K9 Professional Training Series

K9 **Scent Training**
A Manual for Training Your Identification, Tracking and Detection Dog
Resi Gerritsen • Ruud Haak

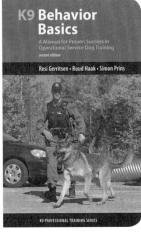

K9 **Behavior Basics**
A Manual for Proven Success in Operational Service Dog Training
second edition
Resi Gerritsen • Ruud Haak • Simon Prins

K9 **Search and Rescue**
A Manual for Training the Natural Way
second edition
Resi Gerritsen • Ruud Haak

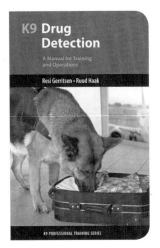

K9 **Drug Detection**
A Manual for Training and Operations
Resi Gerritsen • Ruud Haak

K9 **Explosive and Mine Detection**
A Manual for Training and Operations
Resi Gerritsen • Ruud Haak

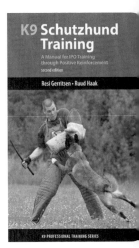

K9 **Schutzhund Training**
A Manual for IPO Training through Positive Reinforcement
second edition
Resi Gerritsen • Ruud Haak

See the complete list at
dogtrainingpress.com